hanuman chalisa

DEMYSTIFYING THE SECRETS

TIMIR NAHA

BlueRose ONE
Stories Matter
NewDelhi • London

BLUEROSE PUBLISHERS
India | U.K.

Copyright © Timir Naha 2025

All rights reserved by author. No part of this publication may be reproduced, stored in a retrieval system or transmitted in any form or by any means, electronic, mechanical, photocopying, recording or otherwise, without the prior permission of the author. Although every precaution has been taken to verify the accuracy of the information contained herein, the publisher assumes no responsibility for any errors or omissions. No liability is assumed for damages that may result from the use of information contained within.

BlueRose Publishers takes no responsibility for any damages, losses, or liabilities that may arise from the use or misuse of the information, products, or services provided in this publication.

For permissions requests or inquiries regarding this publication,
please contact:

BLUEROSE PUBLISHERS
www.BlueRoseONE.com
info@bluerosepublishers.com
+91 8882 898 898
+4407342408967

ISBN: 978-93-6783-211-0

Cover Design: Aman Sharma
Typesetting: Pooja Sharma

First Edition: January 2025

Tribute

This book is humbly dedicated to Shri Neeb Karori Baba,
the embodiment of unconditional love, infinite wisdom,
and boundless grace.

Your life and teachings continue to inspire millions
to walk the path of devotion, service, and selflessness.

Through your blessings, we find strength in Hanuman Ji,
whose infinite power and compassion guide us
to overcome life's challenges and stay rooted in faith.

May this work serve as a humble offering to your legacy
and inspire others to experience the divine within.

Jai Hanuman! Jai Gurudev!

About the Author

Timir Naha is a spiritual seeker and an avid student of the Hanuman Chalisa, having dedicated himself to understanding its deeper meanings.

His journey into the text began with the divine grace of his guru, Shri Neeb Karori Baba, as well as multiple interpretations and sacred writings, drawing from both ancient scriptures and modern spiritual discourses.

A key part of his exploration was visiting revered places such as Kainchi Dham, Ayodhya, and Chitrakoot. These pilgrimages provided Timir with firsthand insights into the profound spiritual significance of Lord Hanuman, allowing him to connect deeply with the divine energy that the Chalisa invokes.

Through these visits, Timir was able to witness the power of devotion and the transformative effects of chanting the Hanuman Chalisa in these sacred locales.

Timir's understanding of the Hanuman Chalisa transcends mere recitation; he has experienced its vibrations and essence in his life, leading him to share his reflections and interpretations for others on a similar spiritual path.

His work serves as a guide for those seeking to understand the profound impact of devotion and strength as embodied by Lord Hanuman.

In addition to his spiritual pursuits, Timir has made significant contributions to the field of English and Writing globally .

His work has garnered recognition, including the prestigious Mahatma Gandhi Samman , awarded to him at the House of Commons, London, for his extraordinary achievements and contributions to society.

His writing continues to inspire, and he has authored several other books that reflect his diverse interests in personal growth, spirituality, and social causes.

Timir's unique blend of spiritual wisdom and professional excellence has made him a respected figure both in the literary world and among those seeking deeper meaning and connection with the divine.

His teachings and writings resonate with individuals on a path to transformation and a more fulfilling life.

Why should read this book?

The Hanuman Chalisa is more than just a hymn—it is a spiritual journey, a timeless guide, and a profound expression of devotion to Lord Hanuman.

Authored by the great saint Goswami Tulsidasji, this spiritual masterpiece transcends the barriers of language, geography, and time to resonate with millions of devotees worldwide. The Chalisa, composed of forty chaupais and two dohas, is an encapsulation of faith, courage, and the power of surrender to the divine.

In the Hanuman Chalisa, Tulsidasji offers vivid descriptions of Lord Hanuman's virtues, recounting his immense strength, unwavering devotion, and unparalleled wisdom.

It is a celebration of his service to Lord Rama, an embodiment of righteousness, and his tireless efforts to restore dharma.

More than just an ode, the Chalisa is a manual for navigating life's trials, urging us to find inspiration in Hanuman's qualities of humility, resilience, and unconditional love.

The Relevance of the Hanuman Chalisa Today

In a world filled with uncertainty, stress, and challenges, the teachings of the Hanuman Chalisa provide solace and strength. Each verse carries a hidden spiritual truth, a lesson in overcoming obstacles, and a reminder of the boundless potential within us when guided by faith.

Lord Hanuman, also known as the Sankat Mochan or the remover of obstacles, is revered not only for his supernatural feats but also for his selflessness and devotion. The Chalisa inspires readers to cultivate these virtues and face life with courage, perseverance, and grace.

The Purpose of This Book

This book is a humble attempt to delve deeper into the meaning and significance of the Hanuman Chalisa. Each chaupai and doha has been explained in detail, offering insights into their linguistic, philosophical, and spiritual essence.

With accompanying glossaries, meanings, and practical applications, this book seeks to bridge the gap between ancient wisdom and contemporary life.

Additionally, this book serves as a tribute to the immeasurable grace of Neeb Karori Baba, my spiritual master who embodied the qualities of compassion, simplicity, and divine connection. His teachings and blessings inspire countless seekers to embrace devotion and the path of service.

For Whom Is This Book?

Whether you are a devotee seeking to deepen your connection with Lord Hanuman, a seeker exploring the spiritual significance of the Hanuman Chalisa, or someone looking for inspiration and guidance, this book is for you. It aims to make the profound wisdom of the Chalisa accessible and relevant to everyone, regardless of their spiritual background.

What Awaits You?

1. A Verse-by-Verse Exploration: Each chaupai and doha is broken down to uncover its meaning, glossary of key terms, and deeper insights.

2. Practical Life Applications: Lessons derived from Hanuman's virtues and stories to inspire action and mindfulness in daily life.

3. Spiritual Secrets: Hidden truths and mystical interpretations of the Chalisa's verses.

4. Insights on Devotion: Reflections on how to embody the spirit of service, humility, and unwavering faith.

5. Connection to the Ramcharitmanas: How the Hanuman Chalisa complements the broader narrative of the Ramayana.

As you embark on this journey, may the grace of Lord Hanuman and the blessings of Neeb Karori Baba guide your path, filling your heart with faith, strength, and divine love.

Contents

Doha 1	1
Doha 2	8
Chaupai 1	14
Chaupai 2	21
Chaupai 3	27
Chaupai 4	34
Chaupai 5	40
Chaupai 6	45
Chaupai 7	51
Chaupai 8	58
Chaupai 9	63
Chaupai 10	68
Chaupai 11	73
Chaupai 12	78
Chaupai 13	84
Chaupai 14	89
Chaupai 15	95
Chaupai 16	100
Chaupai 17	105
Chaupai 18	111
Chaupai 19	117

Chaupai 20	122
Chaupai 21	127
Chaupai 22	133
Chaupai 23	138
Chaupai 24	144
Chaupai 25	149
Chaupai 26	154
Chaupai 27	160
Chaupai 28	166
Chaupai 29	172
Chaupai 30	178
Chaupai 31	183
Chaupai 32	189
Chaupai 33	194
Chaupai 34	199
Chaupai 35	204
Chaupai 36	209
Chaupai 37	215
Chaupai 38	222
Chaupai 39	229
Chaupai 40	236
Doha	242

Doha 1

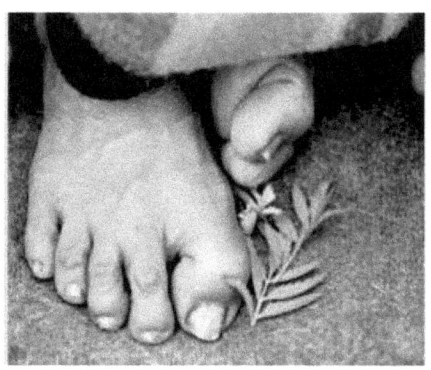

"Shri Guru Charan Saroj Raja Nija Mana Mukura Sudhari,

Baranau Raghubara Bimala Yasha Jo Dayaka Phala Chari."

श्रीगुरु चरन सरोज रज, निज मन मुकुर सुधारि।

बरनऊं रघुबर बिमल जसु, जो दायक फल चारि।।

Glossary of Key Awadhi Words:

1. Shri: A respectful prefix meaning "revered" or "blessed."

2. Guru: Teacher or spiritual guide; one who dispels ignorance (from "gu" = darkness and "ru" = remover).

3. Charan: Feet; symbolic of humility and devotion.

4. Saroj : Lotus; represents purity, detachment, and spiritual elevation.

5. Raja : Dust; signifies the humility of seeking blessings.

6. Nija : One's own or inner.

7. Mana : Mind; the seat of thought and consciousness.

8. Mukura : Mirror; a metaphor for the mind, which reflects truth when cleaned of impurities.

9. Sudhari : Cleansed or purified.

10. Baranau : To describe or extol.

11. Raghubara : Lord Rama; the best of the Raghu dynasty.

12. Bimala : Pure, without blemish.

13. Yasha : Glory or fame.

14. Jo : Who or that which.

15. Dayaka : Giver.

16. Phala : Fruit or reward.

17. Chari : Four; referring to the fourfold goals of human life (Dharma, Artha, Kama, Moksha).

Meaning of the Doha:

"With the dust of the lotus feet of the Guru, I cleanse the mirror of my mind. I extol the pure glory of Lord Rama, who grants the fourfold goals of human life."

The first doha of the Hanuman Chalisa is a gateway to understanding profound spiritual secrets encoded in its verses.

Let us demystify some hidden layers of meaning:

"Shri Guru Charan Saroj Raja Nija Mana Mukura Sudhari"

1. The Secret of the "Dust" (Raja):

The reference to the dust of the Guru's lotus feet is not just symbolic; it is deeply rooted in spiritual philosophy. Dust, often considered insignificant, represents humility. By invoking "Raja," the doha tells us that the smallest aspect of the Guru's teaching—if imbibed sincerely—has the power to transform one's life.

- **Hidden Wisdom:** Dust also symbolizes the accumulation of experience over time. A Guru's "dust" carries the essence of their wisdom and spiritual journey, which can cleanse the karmic layers clouding our mind.

2. The Metaphor of the "Mirror" (Mukura):

The mind, described as a mirror, reflects the world and truth. However, like any mirror, it is prone to gathering "dust" in the form of ignorance, desires, and attachments.

- **Esoteric Insight:** The mirror's cleaning implies the process of self-purification through the Guru's guidance. This purification is akin to spiritual alchemy, transforming the mundane into the divine.

- **Practical Secret:** A purified mind doesn't just reflect truth—it becomes a lens through which one can perceive the divine reality everywhere. This aligns with the Advaitic principle of "Tat Tvam Asi" (You are That).

"Baranau Raghubara Bimala Yasha Jo Dayaka Phala Chari"

बरनऊं रघुबर बिमल जसु, जो दायक फल चारि।

3. The Secret of "Raghubara (Lord Rama):

Lord Rama here is not just the historical prince of Ayodhya but a symbolic representation of paramatma (the Supreme Self).

- **Hidden Meaning :** "Raghubara" also signifies the ultimate light ("Raghu" = rays, "Bara" = supreme), pointing toward the inner divinity that guides us through life's challenges. Chanting Rama's name is said to awaken the dormant divinity within us.

4. The Four Fruits of Life (Phala Chari):

The doha refers to the fourfold objectives of life: Dharma, Artha, Kama, and Moksha. However, these fruits are not just material goals—they are deeply interconnected with spiritual progress.

Spiritual Secret: When pursued under the guidance of the Guru, these objectives become stepping stones toward liberation rather than sources of bondage. For example:

- Dharma leads to self-discipline.

- Artha (wealth) becomes a means of service.

- Kama (desires) transforms into divine longing.

- Moksha is attained not after death but through realizing one's divine nature in this very life.

Deeper Mystical Insights

1. Connection Between Guru and Hanuman:

The Guru in this doha prepares the seeker's mind, but the invocation of Lord Hanuman in the subsequent verses suggests a secret interplay.

Hanuman is the ultimate devotee of Lord Rama and represents perfect surrender, strength, and devotion. This doha subtly implies that once the Guru cleanses our mind, Hanuman takes over to guide us toward divine realization.

2. The Secret of Humility:

This doha emphasizes the transformative power of humility. The seeker bows to the Guru's feet not as a physical act but as a symbolic surrender of ego. The act of cleaning the "mirror" of the mind requires shedding pride, self-centeredness, and preconceived notions.

3. Unlocking Inner Potential:

The reference to "Bimala Yasha" (pure glory) and "Phala Chari" hints at the ultimate realization: all divine virtues and fruits of life are already present within us. The Guru's teachings reveal this hidden truth. The "dust" is merely the illusion that obscures our perception of this inherent divinity.

Ramcharitmanas Connection:

1. Tulsidas's Transformation :

When Tulsidas met his Guru Narharidas, he was consumed by worldly attachments. It was the dust of his Guru's feet—the grace of his teachings—that redirected Tulsidas's love from his wife to Lord Rama, leading to the creation of the Ramcharitmanas and Hanuman Chalisa.

2. Hanuman's Devotion to Rama:

In the Ramayana, Hanuman is the epitome of surrender. When asked who he was, he replied:

- As a body: "I am your servant."

- As a soul: "I am a spark of your divinity."

- As essence: "I am you."

This reflects the ultimate truth revealed through the Guru's guidance—oneness with the divine.

Practical Secrets for Daily Life

1. Start with Humility : Begin every day with gratitude for your teachers, spiritual guides, and life experiences.

2. Chant and Reflect: Recite this doha as a mahamantra, focusing on its meaning to cleanse your mind of distractions.

3. Seek Inner Guidance: Understand that the Guru is not only external but also resides within as your conscience and inner wisdom.

4. Transform Desires : Channel your ambitions toward higher purposes, aligning them with Dharma.

Conclusion:

The first doha of the Hanuman Chalisa encapsulates the journey of spiritual transformation, starting with humility, purification, and devotion. It reminds us that the Guru's grace and the glory of Lord Rama can guide us to realize our true potential and fulfill life's highest objectives. By meditating on this doha, we unlock a roadmap to both worldly success and ultimate liberation.

Doha 2

Buddhi heen tanu janike, sumirau pavana kumar;

Bal buddhi vidya dehu mohi, harahu kalesh vikaar."

बुद्धिहीन तनु जानिके, सुमिरौं पवन कुमार।

बल बुद्धि विद्या देहु मोहिं, हरहु कलेश विकार।।

Glossary of Key Awadhi Words

1. Buddhi: Intellect or wisdom.

2. Heen: Lacking or devoid of.

3. Tanu: Body; represents the seeker's existence.

4. Janike: Knowing or acknowledging.

5. Sumirau: To remember or invoke through prayer.

6. Pavana Kumar: Son of the Wind God (Hanuman).

7. Bal: Strength, both physical and spiritual.

8. Vidya: Knowledge, particularly spiritual wisdom.

9. Dehu : Grant or bestow.

10. Mohi : To me; denotes humility and surrender.

11. Harahu : To remove or dispel.

12. Kalesh : Distress, obstacles, or worldly troubles.

13. Vikaar : Impurities, vices, or internal flaws.

Meaning of the Doha

"Knowing my mind and body to be devoid of wisdom, I invoke the son of the Wind God. Grant me strength, intellect, and knowledge, and remove all my distress and impurities."

Demystifying the Hidden Layers of Meaning

1. The Power of Acknowledging One's Limitations

The Doha begins with the seeker confessing their lack of wisdom and strength. This humble admission is not weakness but an act of surrender to a higher power.

Hidden Secret:

The ego often blocks spiritual progress. By acknowledging limitations, the seeker creates a space for divine intervention, which is the first step toward transformation.

Practical Insight:

Adopt this humility in everyday life. Instead of relying solely on your abilities, invite grace into your challenges by accepting your vulnerabilities.

2. Hanuman as the Source of Divine Energies

Hanuman, the Pavana Kumar, embodies the energies of prana (life force). He symbolizes the awakening of dormant potential within the seeker.

Hidden Secret:

The invocation of Hanuman connects the seeker to their inner strength (bal), higher wisdom (buddhi), and spiritual insight (vidya). This is analogous to balancing the three gunas (qualities):

- Tamas: Transformed into strength.

- Rajas: Directed toward wisdom.

- Sattva: Leads to spiritual enlightenment.

Practical Insight:

Invoke Hanuman through meditation, breath control (pranayama), or chanting the name of Rama to align your energies.

3. The Cleansing of Kalesh and Vikaar

The Doha specifically asks for the removal of two barriers:

- Kalesh: External suffering caused by obstacles and challenges.

- Vikaar: Internal suffering caused by ignorance, ego, and vices.

Hidden Secret:

External and internal challenges are interconnected. By purifying the inner self, the external world reflects harmony. This is akin to the yogic principle that the outer world is a reflection of the inner state.

Practical Insight:

Focus on inner purification through self-discipline and devotion. Reciting the Hanuman Chalisa is an effective tool for removing negative energies.

4. The Prayer for Bal, Buddhi, and Vidya

The seeker asks for three essential attributes:

- Bal: Physical and mental resilience to face challenges.

- Buddhi: Discerning intellect to navigate life wisely.

- Vidya: Spiritual knowledge that leads to liberation.

Hidden Secret :

These three gifts represent the integration of body, mind, and spirit. They correspond to the three stages of spiritual evolution:

- Strength to begin the journey.

- Wisdom to overcome distractions.

- Knowledge to realize the ultimate truth.

Practical Insight:

Incorporate physical strength (exercise), mental clarity (meditation), and spiritual study into your routine to achieve balance.

5. Hanuman as the Archetype of the Ideal Devotee

Hanuman's unwavering devotion to Shri Ram and selfless service make him a role model for seekers.

Hidden Secret:

Hanuman represents the perfect disciple who transforms devotion into divine realization. His qualities—strength, humility, and wisdom—are attainable through disciplined practice and surrender.

Practical Insight:

Emulate Hanuman's qualities in your life. Cultivate humility, practice selfless service, and remain devoted to your higher purpose.

6. The Universal Appeal of the Doha

The prayer in this Doha is universal and applicable to all aspects of life:

- For students, it inspires focus and learning.

- For professionals, it builds resilience and problem-solving skills.

- For spiritual seekers, it aligns the self with the divine.

Hidden Secret:

The Doha encapsulates the essence of Sanatan Dharma—seeking divine grace for personal and spiritual growth. Its beauty lies in its simplicity and universality.

Practical Tips for Daily Life

1. Chant the Doha Daily: Use it as a morning prayer to set the tone for your day.

2. Focus on Balance: Strengthen your body, sharpen your mind, and elevate your soul.

3. Practice Devotion: Dedicate your actions to a higher purpose, following Hanuman's example.

4. Seek Inner Purification: Reflect on your inner vices and work on removing them through self-awareness.

Conclusion

The Doha "Buddhi Heen Tanu Janike" is not merely a prayer but a roadmap to self-transformation. By invoking Hanuman, we awaken our dormant potential, purify our inner and outer worlds, and align ourselves with divine wisdom.

This simple yet profound verse reminds us that strength, wisdom, and knowledge are the keys to overcoming life's challenges and realizing our highest purpose.

Chaupai 1

"Jai Hanuman gyan gun sagar,
Jai kapis tihu lok ujagar."

जय हनुमान ज्ञान गुण सागर।

जय कपीस तिहुँ लोक उजागर।।

Glossary of Key Awadhi Words:

1. Jai: Victory, glory, or praise.

2. Hanuman : The divine monkey god, representing strength, devotion, and wisdom.

3. Gyan: Knowledge or wisdom.

4. Gun: Virtues or qualities.

5. Sagar: Ocean, symbolizing vastness, depth, and abundance.

6. Kapis : Leader of the monkey army; here, it refers to Hanuman.

7. Tihu Lok : The three realms: Swarga (heaven), Prithvi (earth), and Patal (the netherworld).

8. Ujagar : Illuminator, one who brightens or enlightens.

Meaning of the Chaupai:

"Victory to Hanuman, the ocean of wisdom and virtues! Glory to the leader of the monkey army, who is the illuminator of the three worlds."

Hidden Spiritual Secrets:

"Jai Hanuman gyan gun sagar"

- Hanuman as the Ocean of Wisdom and Virtue:

Hanuman is described as *Gyan Gun Sagar*—the ocean of knowledge and virtues. This signifies his infinite capacity for wisdom, knowledge, and exemplary qualities.

Hidden Wisdom:

The ocean symbolizes depth, vastness, and mystery. Just as the ocean has infinite layers, Hanuman's wisdom and virtues are boundless. Through devotion, we too can tap into this vast reservoir of wisdom.

Practical Insight:

Strive to develop both knowledge and virtues. Cultivate wisdom through study and experience, and embody virtues such as humility, courage, and compassion.

-The Connection Between Knowledge and Virtue:

Hanuman's wisdom is not only intellectual but also practical, rooted in righteous action. The perfect balance of intellect and virtue is what gives Hanuman his strength.

Spiritual Secret:

Knowledge without virtue can lead to arrogance, while virtue without knowledge can result in ignorance. True wisdom is the harmonious integration of both.

Practical Insight:

Approach learning and growth with humility, and apply knowledge in a way that aligns with moral and spiritual values.

2. "Jai kapis tihu lok ujagar"

- Hanuman as the Leader of the Monkey Army:

Kapis refers to Hanuman as the leader of the monkey army. Despite his immense strength and wisdom, Hanuman is humble and serves his higher purpose with complete devotion.

Hidden Secret:

Leadership, as demonstrated by Hanuman, is not about dominance but about service, humility, and empowering others. The leader who serves with humility becomes a beacon for others.

Practical Insight:

Whether in a leadership role or in daily life, practice servant leadership—put others first, uplift those around you, and serve with devotion.

- The Illuminator of the Three Worlds :

Hanuman's influence is vast, extending across the three worlds: heaven, earth, and the netherworld. This symbolizes his all-encompassing power to bring light, knowledge, and truth to all realms of existence.

Esoteric Insight :

The three worlds represent different dimensions within each individual:

- Swarga (Heaven) : The mind and intellect, seeking clarity and knowledge.

- Prithvi (Earth) : The body, which needs discipline and strength.

- Patal (Netherworld) : The subconscious, often clouded with fears, doubts, and unresolved emotions.

Hanuman's light illuminates and clears the darkness within these realms.

Practical Insight:

To bring balance to your life, work on illuminating each of these realms. Purify your mind through wisdom, strengthen your body through discipline, and heal your subconscious through meditation and introspection.

Deeper Mystical Insights:

Hanuman as a Symbol of Enlightenment

Hanuman's role as the ujagar (illuminator) of the three worlds shows that true enlightenment is not merely about knowledge but about dispelling ignorance and darkness in every aspect of existence. His light shines through devotion, service, and righteous action.

2. The Power of Service

Hanuman's leadership is grounded in service, not in dominance. This teaches that true power lies in humility and the ability to serve a greater cause. When we serve others selflessly, we align ourselves with higher divine principles.

3. The Three Realms Within Us

The three worlds represent different aspects of the human experience. Hanuman's light reaching each of these realms suggests that enlightenment requires balance in all areas of life—mental, physical, and spiritual.

Ramcharitmanas Connection:

- Hanuman's Role in the Ramayana:

Hanuman's unwavering devotion and service to Lord Rama embody the ideals of devotion, strength, and wisdom. His role as a messenger and servant to Rama illuminates the path of selfless service.

- Tulsidas's Inspiration:

Tulsidas, through his own devotion to Rama, encourages readers to embody Hanuman's virtues—strength, wisdom, and humility—in order to overcome challenges and realize their divine potential.

Practical Application in Daily Life:

1. Cultivate Wisdom and Virtue:

Seek knowledge through study and life experiences, but always align it with virtues such as humility, integrity, and compassion.

2. Serve and Lead with Humility :

Whether in personal or professional settings, embody servant leadership. Focus on uplifting others and serving with devotion.

3. Illuminate the Three Realms Within You:

- Mind : Practice mindfulness and intellectual growth.

- Body : Maintain health and physical discipline.

- Subconscious : Engage in self-reflection and meditation to heal and overcome fears.

4. Bring Light to the World:

Just as Hanuman illuminated the three worlds, bring light into your environment through acts of kindness, sharing knowledge, and supporting others on their spiritual journeys.

Conclusion:

This Chaupai extols Hanuman as the ocean of wisdom and virtues, as well as the illuminator of the three worlds. It highlights the importance of aligning knowledge with virtue, serving with humility, and illuminating all realms of our existence to achieve true spiritual enlightenment.

Chaupai 2

"Ram doot atulit bal dhama,

Anjani putra Pavan sut nama."

राम दूत अतुलित बल धामा।

अंजनि पुत्र पवनसुत नामा।।

Glossary of Key Awadhi Words:

1. Ram doot: Messenger of Lord Rama.

2. Atulit : Incomparable, unmatched.

3. Bal : Strength or power.

4. Dhama : Abode or repository; in this context, a place of extraordinary strength.

5. Anjani : The name of Hanuman's mother, symbolizing divine lineage.

6. Putra: Son.

7. Pavan sut : The son of the wind; referring to Hanuman, whose father is the wind god, Vayu.

Meaning of the Doha:

"Hanuman, the messenger of Lord Rama, is the repository of unparalleled strength. He is the son of Anjani and the wind god, Pavan."

Hidden Spiritual Secrets:

1. "Ram doot atulit bal dhama"

- The Messenger of Lord Rama:

Hanuman is described as the doot (messenger) of Lord Rama, signifying his role as a devoted servant, carrying Rama's message to the world. This highlights the ideal relationship between a devotee and the divine — total submission and service.

Hidden Wisdom:

The role of a doot goes beyond just delivering messages; it involves embodying the values and principles of the one being served. Hanuman's complete surrender to Rama shows how a true messenger must live and breathe the message they carry.

Practical Insight:

We, too, can serve as messengers of truth, compassion, and righteousness by embodying these virtues in our actions and words.

- Incomparable Strength:

Hanuman is not only a messenger but also the repository of atulit bal — incomparable strength. This strength is both physical and spiritual, highlighting Hanuman's role as a protector of dharma and righteousness.

Esoteric Insight:

Hanuman's strength is symbolic of the power we all hold within when aligned with divine purpose. True strength is not just physical might but the power of devotion, faith, and wisdom.

Practical Secret:

In times of struggle, channel your inner strength by connecting with your higher self. Reflect on Hanuman's qualities of resilience and selflessness as tools for overcoming adversity.

2. "Anjani putra Pavan sut nama"

- Son of Anjani and the Wind God:

Hanuman's divine origin is significant: as the son of Anjani (symbolizing purity and devotion) and Pavan (the wind god, symbolizing movement, energy, and life force), he is the embodiment of vitality and devotion.

Hidden Meaning:

Anjani represents purity, and Pavan, the wind, represents energy and force. Hanuman combines these qualities: purity in purpose and the dynamic energy to act on it. The synergy of these forces makes Hanuman unstoppable in his devotion.

Spiritual Secret:

The divine energy in each of us can be awakened by purifying our intentions and focusing our actions towards the greater good, just as Hanuman did with his service to Lord Rama.

Practical Insight:

Align your energy and purpose with a higher spiritual goal. By channeling your energy toward positive action, you can achieve remarkable feats in your personal and spiritual journey.

Deeper Mystical Insights:

1. The Power of Devotion and Service

Hanuman's strength is a reflection of his devotion. His immense physical and spiritual power arises from his total submission to Lord Rama. This serves as a reminder that strength, when used for the service of others, is a divine force.

2. Purity and Divine Energy

Hanuman's parentage represents the harmonious balance of purity (Anjani) and vitality (Pavan). We, too, must seek to purify our intentions and actions while harnessing the energy of the divine to act in the world.

Ramcharitmanas Connection:

- Hanuman as the Ideal Devotee:

Tulsidas presents Hanuman as the perfect disciple, whose life exemplifies the path of devotion. His humility, courage, and unshakable loyalty to Lord Rama set him as a role model for spiritual aspirants.

- Divine Strength and Purpose:

Hanuman's strength and divine origin demonstrate the incredible power that flows when we act with pure intention and in service to a higher cause. This parallels Tulsidas's own spiritual journey, where surrender to the divine leads to divine grace and strength.

Practical Application in Daily Life:

1. Channel Divine Energy:

Just as Hanuman combined divine purity and vitality, you can channel your energy toward your spiritual and personal goals. Focus on service, humility, and positive action.

2. Seek Strength through Devotion:

In moments of doubt, remember that true strength is derived from devotion and alignment with a higher purpose. Like Hanuman, embody the virtues of resilience, humility, and faith.

3. Purify Your Intentions:

Strive to purify your thoughts, words, and actions, aligning them with your spiritual goals. When your intentions are pure, you can harness the divine energy within to overcome any obstacle.

Conclusion:

This Chaupai beautifully encapsulates Hanuman's divine strength and purity of purpose. By embodying his qualities—devotion, humility, and the energy of service—one can align themselves with the higher spiritual force that leads to both personal and spiritual victories.

Chaupai 3

"Mahabir Vikram Bajrangi,

Kumati nivar sumati ke sangi."

महाबीर विक्रम बजरंगी।

कुमति निवार सुमति के संगी।।

Glossary of Key Awadhi Words:

1. Mahabir: The great warrior or mighty hero; refers to Hanuman as a powerful and invincible force.

2. Vikram: Valor, strength, or bravery.

3. Bajrangi: One with a thunderbolt (Bajra) in hand; refers to Hanuman's strength, often associated with the Vajra (a weapon in Hindu mythology), symbolizing indestructibility and power.

4. Kumati: Bad or impure intellect, ignorance, or negative thoughts.

5. Nivar : Removal or destruction.

6. Sumati : Good intellect, wisdom, or positive thoughts.

7. Sangi : Companion or friend.

Meaning of the Chaupai:

"Great warrior, who holds the power of the thunderbolt, Hanuman! You are the remover of bad thoughts and the companion of good intellect and wisdom."

Hidden Spiritual Secrets:

"Mahabir Vikram Bajrangi"

-The Mighty Hero and Warrior:

Hanuman is described as Mahabir (the great warrior) and Vikram (valor or bravery). This speaks to his unparalleled strength and courage, not just physically, but also in spirit. Hanuman's bravery is shown in his selfless service to Lord Rama, facing all obstacles with unwavering resolve.

Hidden Wisdom:

Strength is not only about physical power but also about the inner courage to overcome life's challenges. Hanuman's valor reminds us that true bravery comes from a place of devotion and selflessness.

Practical Insight:

When facing obstacles or fears, channel the courage of Hanuman. Stand firm in your convictions, and let your inner strength carry you through difficulties.

-Thunderbolt Power (Bajrangi):

The term Bajrangi refers to Hanuman's association with the Vajra, a weapon that represents indestructibility. Hanuman's power to destroy evil and protect the righteous is symbolized by the Vajra.

Esoteric Insight:

The Vajra represents the indomitable power of spiritual truth, which cannot be shaken or destroyed. When we align ourselves with this truth, we become impervious to worldly distractions and negative forces.

Practical Secret:

Strengthen your connection to your inner truth and purpose. This will give you resilience in the face of challenges, just as Hanuman's connection to Lord Rama grants him ultimate power.

"Kumati nivar sumati ke sangi"

- Removal of Bad Thoughts (Kumati Nivar):

Hanuman is revered as the one who removes Kumati (bad thoughts or negative intellect). Negative thoughts often stem from ego, ignorance, or unhelpful attachments.

Hanuman's grace dispels these mental afflictions, making way for clarity and peace.

Hidden Meaning:

The mind often carries impurities—such as doubts, fears, and desires—that cloud judgment. Hanuman's energy purifies these negative patterns, replacing them with clarity and righteousness.

Practical Insight:

Whenever you are overwhelmed by negativity or confusion, invoke Hanuman's grace to clear your mind. Meditation, prayer, and positive thinking can help bring clarity and peace to your thoughts.

- Companion of Good Intellect (Sumati ke Sangi):

Hanuman is not only the destroyer of bad intellect but also the companion of Sumati—the intellect that is pure, positive, and wise. This reflects the balance of both intellect and wisdom that Hanuman embodies.

Hidden Wisdom:

True wisdom is not just about intellect; it is the alignment of the intellect with righteousness and purity of thought. Hanuman's intellect is guided by his devotion, making him the perfect embodiment of wisdom.

Practical Secret:

Strive to align your intellectual pursuits with wisdom and compassion. Engage in practices that elevate your thoughts, such as reading sacred texts, meditating, or surrounding yourself with positive influences.

Deeper Mystical Insights:

1. Hanuman as the Protector of the Mind

Hanuman's role as a protector of the mind is emphasized in this Chaupai. His divine energy clears the negative thoughts and afflictions that plague the mind. By invoking Hanuman, we seek not only physical protection but also mental and emotional security.

2. The Balance of Power and Wisdom

Hanuman embodies the perfect balance of Bajrangi (power) and Sumati (wisdom). This duality teaches us that true strength is not just physical, but also mental and spiritual. In life, we must cultivate both qualities to lead a balanced and righteous life.

Ramcharitmanas Connection:

- Hanuman's Role in the Ramayana:

In the Ramayana, Hanuman's valor and wisdom are key to Lord Rama's success in rescuing Sita and defeating Ravana. His bravery is seen in his ability to face overwhelming odds, while his wisdom guides him in making the right choices at critical moments.

- Tulsidas's Depiction of Hanuman:

Tulsidas in his Hanuman Chalisa repeatedly emphasizes Hanuman's strength and wisdom. By invoking these qualities in our lives, we align ourselves with divine protection and guidance.

Practical Application in Daily Life:

1. Invoke Hanuman's Strength:

Call upon Hanuman's strength and bravery when facing challenges. Whether personal, professional, or emotional, draw on his power to overcome obstacles and remain focused.

2. Clear Negative Thoughts:

When negative or impure thoughts arise, consciously let them go. You can chant Hanuman's name or engage in prayer and meditation to clear your mind and restore positive focus.

3. Cultivate Wisdom:

Strive to align your intellect with wisdom and righteousness. Seek knowledge that enriches your life and enhances your understanding of spiritual truths.

4. Balance Power and Wisdom:

Strength and wisdom are two sides of the same coin. Use both to navigate through life's challenges, making sure that your actions are guided by both intellect and heart.

Conclusion:

This Chaupai highlights Hanuman as both the warrior who protects and the wise guide who leads. He dispels negative thoughts and fosters wisdom, offering a holistic approach to spiritual and mental well-being. By invoking his energy, we can strengthen our inner resolve, overcome difficulties, and align our actions with wisdom and righteousness.

Chaupai 4

"Kanchan Baran Viraj Subesa,

Kanan Kundal Kunchit Kesa."

कंचन बरन विराज सुबेसा।

कानन कुण्डल कुँचित केसा।।

Glossary of Key Awadhi Words:

1. Kanchan: Gold; symbolizes purity, brilliance, and divinity.

2. Baran: Color or complexion.

3. Viraj: Radiant, resplendent, or shining.

4. Subesa: Beautiful attire or appearance.

5. Kanan: Earrings.

6. Kundal: Ear ornament; specifically, traditional earrings.

7. Kunchit: Curled or wavy.

8. Kesa: Hair.

Meaning of the Chaupai:

"Your golden complexion shines radiantly, adorned in beautiful attire. You wear earrings, and your hair is curly and lustrous."

Hidden Spiritual Secrets:

1. "Kanchan Baran" – The Golden Complexion

- Symbolism of Gold:

Gold is universally associated with purity, incorruptibility, and brilliance. Hanuman's golden hue represents his divine nature, free of impurities and full of radiant energy.

Hidden Wisdom:

The golden complexion symbolizes the inner purity and spiritual brilliance that a devoted heart reflects. Hanuman's form inspires devotees to cultivate inner purity and truth.

Practical Insight:

Work toward purifying your thoughts and actions, so your inner self reflects divinity like Hanuman's golden hue.

2. "Viraj Subesa" – Radiant and Beautiful Attire

- Subesa Defined:

Hanuman's attire represents not just outer beauty but also the harmony between the inner self and the external actions. His radiant appearance reflects his elevated state of being.

Hidden Wisdom:

True beauty is the expression of inner virtues. Hanuman's appearance teaches that devotion, selflessness, and courage make one truly radiant.

Practical Insight:

Let your actions and demeanor reflect the virtues you carry within. Cultivate kindness, humility, and grace.

3. "Kanan Kundal" – The Earrings

- Significance of Earrings:

Earrings, being close to the ears, symbolize attentiveness and the ability to listen—key virtues of a devoted servant like Hanuman. His adorned ears reflect his readiness to hear and act upon divine will.

Hidden Wisdom:

Just as Hanuman was always attentive to Lord Rama's commands, we must develop the habit of attentive listening—to our conscience, to wise counsel, and to spiritual teachings.

Practical Insight:

Practice active listening in your relationships and spiritual practice. Be receptive to the voice of wisdom and truth.

4. "Kunchit Kesa" - Curly Hair

- The Symbolism of Curly Hair:

Hanuman's curly hair represents his dynamic energy and vibrant personality. It is a mark of vitality, strength, and divine charisma.

Hidden Wisdom:

The waves in his hair mirror the dynamic flow of life and the infinite potential of the divine energy within us. Hanuman teaches us to channel this energy for service and righteousness.

Practical Insight:

Maintain physical vitality and mental agility. Engage in practices like yoga and meditation to harmonize your inner energy with your outer actions.

Deeper Mystical Insights:

1. Outer Form Reflects Inner Virtue

Hanuman's resplendent appearance is a metaphor for his inner purity and devotion. It reminds us that true beauty is the harmony of body, mind, and soul aligned with divine purpose.

2. Dynamic Balance Between Strength and Grace

The combination of golden complexion, radiant attire, and curly hair reflects Hanuman's unique balance of strength and grace—a balance every seeker should aspire to achieve.

3. Devotion Transforms Appearance

Hanuman's beauty is not superficial; it emanates from his devotion to Lord Rama. This teaches that when our lives are centered on higher ideals, we naturally radiate positivity and divine energy.

Ramcharitmanas Connection:

- Hanuman's Role as a Divine Messenger:

Hanuman's glowing appearance is described repeatedly in the Ramayana to emphasize his divinity and the positive energy he brings wherever he goes.

- **Symbolism in Service:**

His radiant form reflects the joy and fulfillment he experiences in serving Lord Rama selflessly.

Practical Application in Daily Life:

1. Cultivate Inner Purity:

Reflect on your thoughts and actions. Strive to remove negativity and align yourself with virtues like devotion and compassion.

2. Radiate Positivity:

Let your inner state influence your outer demeanor. Greet life's challenges with a smile and grace, just as Hanuman's radiant form embodies positivity.

3. Stay Attentive and Receptive:

Like Hanuman's adorned ears, be an active listener. Pay attention to spiritual teachings and wise counsel.

4. Channel Dynamic Energy:

Maintain physical and mental vitality to face life's challenges with strength and grace, just as Hanuman does.

Conclusion:

This Chaupai highlights Hanuman's divine beauty and energy, which are reflections of his pure devotion and virtues. It inspires us to cultivate inner purity, harmony, and vitality, allowing us to radiate positivity in our own lives.

Chaupai 5

"Hath Bajra o Dhvaja Viraje,

Kandhe Munj Janeo Saaje."

हाथ बज्र औ ध्वजा विराजे।

काँधे मुँज जनेऊ साजे।।

Glossary of Key Awadhi Words:

1. Hath: Hand.

2. Bajra: Thunderbolt; the weapon of Lord Indra, symbolizing strength and invincibility.

3. Dhvaja: Flag or banner; a symbol of honor and purpose.

4. Viraje: Adorned or placed in splendor.

5. Kandhe : Shoulder.

6. Munj: A type of sacred grass used to make the yajnopavita (sacred thread).

7. Janeo : Sacred thread worn by initiates of Vedic traditions, symbolizing spiritual responsibility.

8. Saaje : Dressed or adorned.

Meaning of the Chaupai :

"In your hand, you hold the thunderbolt and the flag, and your shoulder is adorned with the sacred thread made of *munj* grass."

Hidden Spiritual Secrets:

1. "Hath Bajra" – The Thunderbolt in Hand

- Symbolism of the Thunderbolt:

The thunderbolt (Bajra) signifies unshakable strength, courage, and decisiveness. It is a weapon of divine justice, symbolizing Hanuman's ability to destroy ignorance and evil.

Hidden Wisdom:

The thunderbolt also represents focused action and willpower. Hanuman wields it to uphold dharma and eliminate obstacles.

Practical Insight:

Cultivate unwavering determination and strength in the face of adversity. Like Hanuman, focus your energy on righteous goals.

2. "Dhvaja Viraje" – The Flag or Banner

- Symbolism of the Flag:

The dhvaja represents purpose, honor, and leadership. Hanuman carries it as a symbol of his unwavering devotion to Lord Rama and his mission to uphold righteousness.

Hidden Wisdom:

The flag is a call to align one's life with higher ideals and to serve as a beacon of inspiration for others.

Practical Insight:

Define a higher purpose for your life. Let your actions inspire others to pursue truth and righteousness.

3. "Kandhe Munj Janeo Saaje" – The Sacred Thread on the Shoulder

- Significance of the Sacred Thread:

The janeu represents spiritual initiation and responsibility. It symbolizes Hanuman's adherence to dharma, self-discipline, and his role as a protector of sacred values.

Hidden Wisdom:

The janeu reminds us of the spiritual commitment required to walk the path of righteousness. It also emphasizes the balance between worldly duties and spiritual aspirations.

Practical Insight:

Take responsibility for your spiritual growth. Uphold ethical values and maintain discipline in daily life.

Deeper Mystical Insights:

1. Balancing Strength and Spirituality

Hanuman's adornments reflect a harmonious blend of physical power (bajra) and spiritual dedication (janeu). This balance is essential for a fulfilling life.

2. A Symbol of Leadership

By carrying the flag, Hanuman embodies leadership rooted in service and devotion. His role inspires us to lead with humility and a sense of responsibility toward a higher cause.

3. Sacred Responsibility

The sacred thread signifies that true power comes with responsibility. Hanuman's actions remind us that strength should be used for service, not personal gain.

Ramcharitmanas Connection:

- Hanuman as the Perfect Servant:

Hanuman's adornments emphasize his readiness to serve Lord Rama with all his might and devotion. His janeu symbolizes his unwavering commitment to dharma.

- The Ideal Warrior:

By holding the thunderbolt and flag, Hanuman reflects the qualities of an ideal warrior who fights for truth and justice.

Practical Application in Daily Life:

1. Cultivate Strength and Focus:

Like Hanuman with his thunderbolt, channel your inner strength to overcome challenges and eliminate negativity.

2. Define Your Purpose:

Carry your own "flag" by aligning your actions with a clear purpose or goal that serves a higher ideal.

3. Embrace Spiritual Responsibility:

Reflect on your ethical and spiritual responsibilities. Commit to living a disciplined and value-driven life.

4. Lead with Humility:

Use your talents and abilities not for personal gain but for the betterment of others, as Hanuman does.

Conclusion:

This Chaupai highlights Hanuman's strength, leadership, and spiritual commitment. It reminds us to balance power with responsibility, purpose with humility, and action with devotion. By embodying these qualities, we can lead a life of service and righteousness.

Chaupai 6

"Sankar Suvan Kesaeri Nandan,

Tej Pratap Maha Jag Vandan."

शंकर सुवन केसरी नंदन।

तेज प्रताप महा जग वंदन।।

Glossary of Key Awadhi Words:

1. Sankar: Lord Shiva, representing the destroyer in the Hindu trinity.

2. Suvan : Son or manifestation.

3. Kesaeri: Refers to Kesari, Hanuman's father, a noble and valiant monkey chief.

4. Nandan : Beloved son.

5. Tej : Radiance, brilliance, or divine energy.

6. Pratap : Valor, might, or splendor.

7. Maha : Great or supreme.

8. Jag : The world or universe.

9. Vandan : Adoration or reverence.

Meaning of the Chaupai:

"You are the son of Lord Shiva and Kesari, endowed with immense radiance and valor, and revered throughout the world."

Hidden Spiritual Secrets:

1. "Sankar Suvan" – Manifestation of Shiva

- Divine Connection to Lord Shiva:

Hanuman is described as the son of Lord Shiva, emphasizing his divine origin. He embodies Shiva's energy (Shakti), strength, and unwavering focus, making him a symbol of transformation and spiritual power.

Hidden Wisdom:

As the son of Shiva, Hanuman represents the destruction of ignorance (*avidya*) and the awakening of higher consciousness.

Practical Insight:

Invoke Hanuman to overcome ignorance and tap into your inner strength for spiritual growth and transformation.

2. "Kesaeri Nandan" – Son of Kesari

- Worldly Heritage:

As the son of Kesari, a noble and valiant leader of the monkey clan, Hanuman also inherits worldly virtues such as courage, loyalty, and leadership.

Hidden Wisdom:

This dual heritage (divine and worldly) signifies the harmony between spiritual divinity and earthly responsibility.

Practical Insight:

Recognize your spiritual essence while honoring your worldly duties. Balance both aspects for a fulfilling life.

3. "Tej Pratap" – Radiance and Valor

- Tej (Radiance):

Hanuman's brilliance reflects his divine energy, which lights up the darkest corners of the world and dispels ignorance.

- **Pratap (Valor):**

His courage and might are unparalleled, symbolizing his readiness to protect and uphold dharma at all costs.

Hidden Wisdom:

Radiance (Tej) comes from inner purity, while valor (Pratap) arises from selfless devotion to a higher cause.

Practical Insight:

Cultivate inner purity and courage to face challenges in life. Shine brightly by aligning your actions with truth and righteousness.

4. "Maha Jag Vandan" – Revered by the World

- **Universal Reverence:**

Hanuman's qualities make him beloved and venerated across the world. His deeds inspire devotion, respect, and admiration from all beings.

Hidden Wisdom:

True reverence arises when one lives a life of selfless service, humility, and unwavering faith.

Practical Insight:

Strive to be a source of inspiration for others by embodying virtues like selflessness, strength, and humility.

Deeper Mystical Insights:

1. Hanuman as the Bridge Between Shiva and Vishnu

Hanuman, being a manifestation of Shiva, serves Lord Rama, an incarnation of Vishnu. This reflects the harmony between two aspects of divinity—destruction (Shiva) and preservation (Vishnu).

2. Radiance as Inner Divinity

The brilliance (Tej) attributed to Hanuman is not merely physical but represents the divine light within every being. By cleansing the mind and heart, this light can shine forth.

3. Valor Rooted in Devotion

Hanuman's courage is fueled by his devotion to Lord Rama. His strength comes from his complete surrender to the divine will, teaching us that true valor is rooted in faith and purpose.

Ramcharitmanas Connection:

- Shiva's Boon:

It is believed that Lord Shiva blessed Hanuman's mother, Anjana, with a son who would be his divine manifestation. This lineage reflects Hanuman's role as a protector of dharma and destroyer of ignorance.

- **Hanuman's Radiance in Lanka:**

When Hanuman sets Lanka ablaze, his radiance illuminates the darkness, symbolizing the triumph of truth over deceit.

Practical Application in Daily Life:

1. Balance Divinity and Responsibility:

Like Hanuman, acknowledge your spiritual essence while fulfilling your worldly duties with dedication and courage.

2. Cultivate Inner Radiance:

Purify your thoughts, actions, and intentions to allow your inner light to shine brightly.

3. Embody Courage and Service:

Let your strength and valor serve a higher purpose. Stand up for what is right, even in the face of adversity.

4. Seek Universal Goodwill:

Live a life of humility and service to earn respect and reverence from others, just as Hanuman is adored universally.

Conclusion:

This Chaupai highlights Hanuman's divine and earthly lineage, his brilliance and courage, and his universal reverence. It inspires us to embody these qualities in our own lives, balancing spiritual growth with worldly responsibilities and serving as a beacon of strength and humility.

Chaupai 7

"Vidyavan Guni Ati Chatur,

Ram Kaj Karibe Ko Atur."

विद्यावान गुनी अतिचतुर।

राम काज करिबे को अतुर।।

Glossary of Key Awadhi Words

1. Vidyavan: Knowledgeable or learned.

2. Guni: Virtuous, possessing noble qualities.

3. Ati: Extremely or exceedingly.

4. Chatur : Clever, wise, or intelligent.

5. Ram : Refers to Lord Rama, the epitome of dharma and virtue.

6. Kaj : Work, task, or service.

7. Karibe: To perform or accomplish.

8. Ko Atur : Eager or enthusiastic.

Meaning of the Chaupai

"Hanuman is highly knowledgeable, virtuous, and supremely intelligent. He is always eager and enthusiastic to accomplish Lord Rama's tasks."

Hidden Spiritual Secrets

1. Vidyavan: Embodiment of Knowledge

- Hanuman's Knowledge :

Hanuman is a master of scriptures, linguistics, and wisdom. His knowledge goes beyond mere intellectual understanding, encompassing spiritual insights and practical application.

Hidden Wisdom:

Knowledge (Vidya) without purpose or direction is incomplete. Hanuman's wisdom is dedicated to serving a higher cause, symbolizing the ideal use of knowledge.

Practical Insight:

Pursue knowledge not just for personal gain but to contribute to the greater good. Align your learning with service and compassion.

2. Guni: Possessor of Virtues

- **Noble Qualities of Hanuman:**

Hanuman is the embodiment of humility, devotion, courage, and compassion. These virtues make him not only a powerful being but also a deeply compassionate and relatable figure.

Hidden Wisdom:

Virtues are the foundation of true greatness. Knowledge without virtues leads to arrogance, while virtues without knowledge can lack direction.

Practical Insight:

Cultivate virtues alongside knowledge to achieve harmony and balance in life.

3. Ati Chatur: Supreme Intelligence

- **Hanuman's Cleverness:**

Hanuman's intelligence is not only academic but also practical. His quick thinking and strategic planning are evident in his exploits, such as finding Sita in Lanka and setting Ravana's city ablaze.

Hidden Wisdom:

Intelligence is most effective when combined with intuition and divine alignment. Hanuman's cleverness serves his devotion to Rama, ensuring his actions are purposeful.

Practical Insight:

Use intelligence and resourcefulness to overcome challenges, especially when serving a noble cause.

4. Ram Kaj Karibe Ko Atur: Devotion in Action

- Eagerness to Serve Lord Rama:

Hanuman's devotion is not passive; it is active and enthusiastic. His sole purpose is to serve Lord Rama and uphold dharma, without any hesitation or delay.

Hidden Wisdom:

True devotion is expressed through selfless action. Serving a higher purpose with eagerness and sincerity is the hallmark of a devotee.

Practical Insight:

Approach your responsibilities and acts of service with enthusiasm, treating them as opportunities to honor the divine.

Deeper Mystical Insights

1. Knowledge, Virtue, and Intelligence as Pillars of Dharma

Hanuman integrates these three qualities seamlessly. Together, they make him an ideal servant of Lord Rama and a symbol of the perfect balance between intellect, morality, and devotion.

2. Enthusiasm as a Divine Quality

Hanuman's eagerness reflects his alignment with divine will. When one is connected to a higher purpose, enthusiasm flows naturally, dispelling doubt and hesitation.

3. Hanuman as the Ideal Disciple

Hanuman embodies the qualities of an ideal student and devotee—endlessly learning, cultivating virtues, and applying wisdom in service.

Ramcharitmanas Connection

- Hanuman's Eagerness to Serve:

Throughout the Ramcharitmanas, Hanuman demonstrates an unparalleled zeal to serve Lord Rama. From leaping across the ocean to find Sita to carrying the Sanjeevani herb to save Lakshmana, his actions reflect his unwavering commitment.

- **Lesson from Sugriva's Court:**

When Hanuman first meets Rama, he recognizes his divine nature immediately and offers his services without hesitation, exemplifying his intelligence and devotion.

Practical Application in Daily Life

1. Pursue Knowledge with Purpose:

Learn continuously, but let your knowledge guide you toward serving others and uplifting society.

2. Cultivate Virtues:

Balance your intellectual pursuits with humility, compassion, and integrity.

3. Use Intelligence Wisely :

Apply your intelligence to solve problems and support causes that align with your values and principles.

4. Serve Enthusiastically :

Whatever tasks you undertake, approach them with enthusiasm and dedication, treating them as acts of devotion.

5. Align with a Higher Purpose:

Like Hanuman, dedicate your actions to a purpose greater than yourself, and let this guide your decisions and efforts.

Conclusion

This Chaupai highlights Hanuman's unparalleled qualities—his wisdom, virtues, and intelligence—and his unwavering eagerness to serve Lord Rama. It inspires us to cultivate these attributes and approach life with a sense of devotion, purpose, and enthusiasm.

Chaupai 8

Prabhu Charitra Sunibe Ko Rasiya,

Ram Lakhan Sita Man Basiya.

प्रभु चरित्र सुनिबे को रसिया।

राम लखन सीता मन बसिया।।

Glossary of Key Awadhi Words

1. Prabhu : Lord or master; refers to Lord Rama.

2. Charitra : Deeds, character, or divine exploits.

3. Sunibe Ko : To hear or listen to.

4. Rasiya : Connoisseur or one who takes great joy in something.

5. Ram : Lord Rama, symbolizing righteousness and virtue.

6. Lakhan : Lakshmana, Rama's devoted brother, symbolizing loyalty and service.

7. Sita : Consort of Lord Rama, representing purity, grace, and devotion.

8. Man Basiya : Resides in the heart or mind.

Meaning of the Chaupai

"Hanuman delights in listening to the divine exploits of Lord Rama. He holds Rama, Lakshmana, and Sita deeply within his heart."

Hidden Spiritual Secrets

1. Prabhu Charitra Sunibe Ko Rasiya: Joy in Devotion

Hanuman is described as someone who derives immense joy and satisfaction from listening to the divine stories of Lord Rama. This signifies his deep devotion and connection to the divine.

Hidden Wisdom :

Listening to the stories of divine beings or spiritual masters not only brings joy but also inspires and elevates the listener's consciousness.

Practical Insight :

Engage regularly in activities like reading scriptures, attending satsangs (spiritual gatherings), or meditating on the lives of great beings to find inspiration and inner peace.

2. Ram Lakhan Sita Man Basiya: The Divine in the Heart

Hanuman carries the divine trio—Rama, Lakshmana, and Sita—in his heart, symbolizing his unwavering devotion and spiritual alignment.

Hidden Wisdom:

To keep the divine within one's heart means to align thoughts, words, and actions with dharma (righteousness), selflessness, and compassion.

Practical Insight:

Make space in your heart for divine qualities like love, courage, and humility. Visualize carrying these virtues with you in all situations.

Deeper Mystical Insights

1. The Power of Listening

In spiritual traditions, listening (Shravana) is considered the first step toward self-realization. Hanuman's joy in listening to Rama's exploits shows that spiritual growth begins with an open and receptive mind.

2. The Divine Trio as Archetypes

- Rama: The ideal self, representing truth and dharma.

- Lakshmana : The loyal companion, symbolizing discipline and service.

- Sita : The soul's purity and devotion.

By holding these archetypes in his heart, Hanuman exemplifies the harmony of truth, service, and love.

3. Inner Abode of the Divine

Hanuman reminds us that divinity is not external but resides within. To realize this, one must cleanse the heart through devotion and righteous living.

Ramcharitmanas Connection

- Hanuman's Role in the Ramayana:

Hanuman is not only a servant of Lord Rama but also an admirer of his virtues. His love for listening to Rama's stories reinforces the importance of connecting with divine wisdom through devotion.

- In Lanka :

While searching for Sita, Hanuman carries the image of Rama, Lakshmana, and Sita in his heart, drawing strength from their presence. This unwavering focus helps him overcome challenges.

Practical Application in Daily Life

1. Immerse Yourself in Inspiring Stories

Just as Hanuman delights in Rama's exploits, find joy in stories that inspire and uplift you, whether they are spiritual or motivational.

2. Carry the Divine in Your Heart

Keep your values and higher purpose close to your heart. Let them guide your actions and decisions.

3. Practice Devotion Through Listening

Develop the habit of listening to spiritual discourses or engaging in meaningful conversations that enrich your soul.

4. Make Your Heart a Divine Abode

Create a mental space for qualities like love, compassion, and truth to reside within you, making your heart a sanctuary for positivity.

Conclusion

This Chaupai beautifully illustrates Hanuman's deep devotion and the joy he derives from listening to the divine exploits of Rama. It encourages us to keep divinity in our hearts and find inspiration in spiritual teachings, reminding us that true joy and strength come from staying connected to the divine.

Chaupai 9

Sukshma Rupa Dhari Siyaha Dikhava,

Vikat Rupa Dhari Lanka Jarava.

सूक्ष्म रूप धरी सियाहि दिखावा।

विकट रूप धरी लंका जरावा।।

Glossary of Key Awadhi Words

1. Sukshma : Subtle, small, or delicate.

2. Rupa : Form or appearance.

3. Dhari : To assume or take on.

4. Siyaha : A Brahmin or scholar, often representing a form of gentleness or wisdom.

5. Dikhava : To reveal or show.

6. Vikat : Fierce, terrifying, or powerful.

7. Lanka : The kingdom of Ravana, symbolic of ego, pride, and unrighteousness.

8. Jarava : To burn or destroy.

Meaning of the Chaupai

"Assuming a subtle form, Hanuman appeared before Sita in Ashok Vatika. Taking a fierce form, he burned Lanka to the ground."

Hidden Spiritual Secrets

1. Sukshma Rupa Dhari Siyaha Dikhava

- Gentleness in Approach :

Hanuman's subtle form represents his wisdom and humility. While delivering Rama's message to Sita, he approached her in a gentle and non-threatening manner to reassure her of Rama's love and his mission to rescue her.

Hidden Wisdom:

In delicate situations, adopting a gentle and wise approach often yields the best results.

Practical Insight :

When dealing with sensitive matters, act with care, humility, and empathy to foster understanding and trust.

2. Vikat Rupa Dhari Lanka Jarava

- Fierceness in Righteous Action :

Hanuman's fierce form symbolizes his strength and determination. By burning Lanka, he destroyed the hub of unrighteousness, symbolizing the annihilation of ego, pride, and evil.

Hidden Wisdom :

While gentleness is essential, there are times when fierce action is necessary to confront injustice or protect dharma.

Practical Insight :

Face challenges and injustices with courage. Be gentle when needed but firm and decisive when righteousness is at stake.

Deeper Mystical Insights

1. Dual Nature of Hanuman

Hanuman's ability to shift between subtlety and fierceness reflects the balance between compassion and strength that every individual should strive for in life.

- Sukshma Rupa : Represents the inner strength of wisdom, patience, and humility.

- Vikat Rupa : Represents external strength, courage, and action.

2. Burning Lanka as a Symbol

Lanka, as the seat of Ravana's pride and ego, symbolizes the inner stronghold of negative traits like greed, arrogance, and delusion. Hanuman's act of burning Lanka signifies the purification process required to destroy these vices within ourselves.

Ramcharitmanas Connection

- Reaching Sita in Ashok Vatika :

Hanuman's subtle form enabled him to enter Ravana's heavily guarded kingdom and deliver Rama's message to Sita, demonstrating his intelligence and devotion.

- Burning Lanka:

After being captured by Ravana and setting his tail aflame, Hanuman turned this into an opportunity to destroy Lanka, proving that even adversities can be used as tools for righteous purposes.

Practical Application in Daily Life

1. Adapt Your Approach :

Be gentle when the situation demands empathy and understanding, but be assertive when confronting wrongdoing or protecting what's right.

2. Destroy Inner Lanka :

Identify and address negative traits within yourself—like ego, pride, and anger—through self-reflection and discipline.

3. Turn Adversity Into Opportunity :

When faced with challenges, channel your inner strength to overcome them and use them as stepping stones for personal growth.

4. Balance Compassion and Strength:

Strive to cultivate a balance of inner wisdom and outer courage in your interactions and decisions.

Conclusion

This Chaupai highlights Hanuman's versatility and profound wisdom. It teaches us to adapt to circumstances by balancing gentleness with strength, using each quality in service of dharma. Hanuman's actions remind us of the importance of righteous living and the courage to confront challenges while remaining humble and compassionate.

Chaupai 10

Bhim Rup Dhari Asur Sanhare,

Ram Chandra Ke Kaaj Saware.

भीम रूप धरी असुर संहारे।

रामचंद्र के काज संवारे।।

Glossary of Key Awadhi Words

1. Bhim : Gigantic, powerful, or immense.

2. Rup : Form or appearance.

3. Dhari : To assume or take on.

4. Asur : Demons, representing unrighteousness and evil.

5. Sanhare : To destroy or annihilate.

6. Ram Chandra : Lord Rama, the epitome of dharma and virtue.

7. Kaaj : Task, mission, or duty.

8. Saware : To accomplish, complete, or perfect.

Meaning of the Chaupai

"Assuming a powerful form, Hanuman destroyed the demons and successfully accomplished Lord Rama's mission."

Hidden Spiritual Secrets

Bhim Rup Dhari Asur Sanhare

- Power Unleashed for Righteousness :

Hanuman's Bhim Rup represents his immense strength, both physical and spiritual. He used this form not for personal gain but to destroy the forces of evil Asur, upholding dharma.

Hidden Wisdom :

Strength and power are tools to be used in service of justice and righteousness, not for self-serving purposes.

Practical Insight :

Channel your energy and resources to combat negativity, protect the vulnerable, and foster fairness in your surroundings.

2. Ram Chandra Ke Kaaj Saware

- Service to the Divine Will :

Every action of Hanuman is aligned with fulfilling Lord Rama's mission, symbolizing devotion and selfless service. He embodies the ideal servant of the divine, prioritizing duty over personal desires.

Hidden Wisdom :

Aligning one's actions with a higher purpose brings fulfillment and ensures success in life's endeavors.

Practical Insight :

Dedicate your actions to a noble cause or higher purpose. Let devotion, discipline, and duty guide your efforts.

Deeper Mystical Insights

1. The Dual Role of Strength

Hanuman's ability to shift between gentleness and ferocity demonstrates the dual nature of strength:

- Inner Strength: The capacity for patience, resilience, and devotion.

- Outer Strength : The courage and power to act decisively when faced with adversity.

2. The Symbolism of Destroying Demons

The Asurs represent inner demons—fear, anger, greed, and ignorance. Hanuman's destruction of these forces symbolizes the inner purification necessary for spiritual growth and alignment with divine will.

3. Fulfillment Through Selfless Service

By dedicating his immense power to Lord Rama's mission, Hanuman shows that true fulfillment lies in serving a higher cause. His unwavering commitment is a lesson in loyalty and purpose-driven action.

Ramcharitmanas Connection

- Defeating Ravana's Army:

Hanuman's Bhim Rup was instrumental during battles, showcasing his physical might and strategic brilliance in overcoming evil forces.

- Sundar Kand:

Hanuman's journey to Lanka and his deeds there, including the destruction of demons, are central to his role in advancing Lord Rama's mission to rescue Sita and restore dharma.

Practical Application in Daily Life

1. Use Your Strength Wisely:

Identify your strengths—whether physical, intellectual, or emotional—and use them to protect, uplift, and serve others.

2. Confront Your Inner Demons :

Recognize and work on overcoming negative tendencies like ego, fear, or anger through self-discipline and mindfulness.

3. Serve a Noble Purpose:

Dedicate your actions to a cause greater than yourself, whether it's supporting family, contributing to society, or pursuing spiritual growth.

4. Balance Inner and Outer Power:

Develop both internal resilience and the external courage to face challenges with clarity and determination.

Conclusion

This Chaupai exemplifies Hanuman's unwavering commitment to dharma and his use of immense power to serve a noble cause. It inspires us to align our strength and actions with higher purposes, teaching that true greatness lies in selfless service and righteous action.

Chaupai 11

Lay Sajeevan Lakhan Jiyay,

Shri Raghubar Harshi Ur Lay.

लाय सजीवन लखन जियाए।

श्रीरघुबीर हरषि उर लाए।।

Glossary of Key Awadhi Words

1. Lay : Brought or fetched.

2. Sajeevan : Refers to the Sanjeevani Booti, the life-restoring herb.

3. Lakhan : Lakshman, Lord Rama's devoted brother.

4. Jiyay : Revived or brought back to life.

5. Shri Raghubar : Lord Rama, the best among the Raghu dynasty.

6. Harshi : Delighted or filled with joy.

7. Ur : Heart.

8. Lay : Held or embraced.

Meaning of the Chaupai

"Hanuman brought the Sanjeevani Booti to revive Lakshman, and Lord Rama joyfully embraced him to his heart."

Hidden Spiritual Secrets

1. Lay Sajeevan Lakhan Jiyay

- Symbol of Life-Giving Power:

The Sanjeevani Booti represents the divine power of restoration and rejuvenation. Hanuman's unwavering focus and determination to retrieve it illustrate his role as a savior and restorer of hope.

Hidden Wisdom:

Just as the Sanjeevani Booti restored life to Lakshman, acts of service, devotion, and compassion can revive the spirits of those in despair.

Practical Insight:

Be a source of healing and support for others. Whether through kind words or actions, your efforts can uplift those in need.

2. Shri Raghubar Harshi Ur Lay

- Lord Rama's Joyful Embrace :

Rama's delight in Hanuman's success reflects the divine's boundless love for devoted service. It signifies the ultimate reward of devotion—being united with the divine.

Hidden Wisdom:

God embraces those who selflessly serve with unwavering faith and dedication, showing that divine grace flows naturally to those who act in righteousness.

Practical Insight:

Offer your work as devotion to a higher purpose. Fulfillment lies in knowing you've contributed meaningfully to the well-being of others.

Deeper Mystical Insights

1. The Journey to Find the Sanjeevani Booti

Hanuman's challenging journey to the Dronagiri Mountain symbolizes the seeker's determination to overcome obstacles in pursuit of spiritual enlightenment or solutions to life's problems.

2. The Power of Faith and Determination

Hanuman did not let uncertainty about the specific herb deter him. His decision to carry the entire mountain reflects unyielding faith and a "whatever it takes" mindset in fulfilling his mission.

3. Divine Reciprocity

Lord Rama's embrace signifies the culmination of service and devotion. The union of the divine and the devotee represents the ultimate spiritual goal—oneness with the divine.

Ramcharitmanas Connection

- Lakshman's Revival:

During the battle with Ravana, Lakshman was struck unconscious. Hanuman's retrieval of the Sanjeevani Booti highlights his pivotal role in sustaining the mission of Lord Rama and restoring hope in dire moments.

- Sundar Kand :

Hanuman's extraordinary feats in the Ramayana showcase his strength, devotion, and ability to triumph over seemingly insurmountable challenges.

Practical Application in Daily Life

1. Be a Source of Life and Hope:

Just as Hanuman brought life back to Lakshman, seek to uplift others through acts of kindness, support, and encouragement.

2. Stay Focused on Your Mission:

Despite challenges or uncertainty, remain committed to your goals, especially when they benefit others.

3. Seek the Divine Embrace :

Offer your actions as service to a higher power, knowing that the reward is the joy and fulfillment of divine connection.

4. Embody Resilience:

Hanuman's determination to find the Sanjeevani Booti teaches us to persist, even when the path is unclear. Challenges are stepping stones to success.

Conclusion

This Chaupai celebrates Hanuman's unparalleled devotion and determination, teaching us the importance of selflessness, resilience, and faith in service to a higher cause. Lord Rama's joyous embrace signifies the ultimate reward of aligning our actions with divine will.

Chaupai 12

Raghupati Kinhi Bahut Badai,

Tum Mam Priya Bharat Hi Sam Bhai.

रघुपति किन्ही बहुत बड़ाई।

तुम मम प्रिय भरतहि सम भाई।।

Glossary of Key Awadhi Words

1. Raghupati : Lord Rama, the leader of the Raghu dynasty.

2. Kinhi : Did or offered.

3. Bahut : Much or great.

4. Badai : Praise or admiration.

5. Tum : You, referring to Hanuman.

6. Mam : Me or mine, spoken by Lord Rama.

7. Priya : Dear or beloved.

8. Bharat : Lord Rama's younger brother, known for his unwavering devotion and selflessness.

9. Hi : Indeed, emphasizing a statement.

10. Sam : Equal or comparable.

11. Bhai : Brother.

Meaning of the Chaupai

"Lord Rama praised you greatly and declared, 'You are as dear to me as my own brother Bharat.'"

Hidden Spiritual Secrets

1. Raghupati Kinhi Bahut Badai

The Power of Selfless Service :

Lord Rama's immense praise for Hanuman highlights the divine acknowledgment of pure, devoted service. Hanuman's deeds were driven not by ego but by devotion, which made his service exemplary.

Hidden Wisdom:

True greatness lies in selfless acts. When performed with sincerity, even the smallest efforts earn divine favor and blessings.

Practical Insight:

Dedicate your actions to a higher purpose, free from the expectation of rewards. Service with love and humility always attracts appreciation and grace.

2. Tum Mam Priya Bharat Hi Sam Bhai

- Comparison to Bharat :

Bharat's devotion to Lord Rama is legendary. Despite being offered the throne, he chose to rule Ayodhya as Rama's steward, placing Rama's sandals on the throne. By equating Hanuman to Bharat, Lord Rama underscores Hanuman's unparalleled loyalty and love.

Hidden Wisdom:

Hanuman and Bharat both embody unwavering devotion, humility, and selflessness—qualities that endear them to the divine. Their examples teach us the essence of true devotion: prioritizing the divine will above personal desires.

Practical Insight:

Foster a sense of devotion and selflessness in your relationships and responsibilities. Treat every task as an offering to something greater than yourself.

Deeper Mystical Insights

1. Hanuman as the Divine Servant

Lord Rama's acknowledgment of Hanuman's unparalleled dedication reinforces the idea that selfless service bridges the gap between the individual soul (jivatma) and the supreme soul (paramatma).

2. Bharat and Hanuman: Archetypes of Devotion

Bharat represents love and sacrifice for Rama from a familial perspective, while Hanuman exemplifies devotion through action and service. Together, they embody the full spectrum of devotion.

3. Divine Love Transcends Roles

Rama's declaration reflects that divine love is not limited to family ties. It is accessible to anyone who serves with sincerity and devotion.

Ramcharitmanas Connection

- **Bharat's Devotion :**

When Rama was exiled to the forest, Bharat chose to live a life of austerity in Nandigram, symbolizing his deep love and respect for Rama.

- **Hanuman's Devotion:**

Hanuman's role in uniting Rama with Sita and aiding in the war against Ravana demonstrates devotion through tireless action and commitment.

Practical Application in Daily Life

1. Embrace Selfless Service:

Imitate Hanuman's unwavering devotion in your work and relationships. Approach every task with humility and a sense of purpose.

2. Learn from Bharat's Sacrifice:

Let go of personal gain in favor of greater values and higher ideals. Prioritize love, respect, and duty over selfish desires.

3. Seek Divine Acknowledgment:

Focus on doing good for its own sake, trusting that true acknowledgment comes from within and above.

4. Cultivate Devotional Balance:

Combine Bharat's reflective love and Hanuman's active service in your spiritual and personal endeavors to create a balanced approach to life.

Conclusion

This Chaupai reflects the profound bond between the divine and the devotee. By comparing Hanuman to Bharat, Lord Rama highlights the pinnacle of devotion, humility, and selfless service. It reminds us that dedication to higher ideals elevates us in the eyes of the divine.

Chaupai 13

Sahas Badan Tumharo Yash Gaave,

Asa Kahi Shripati Kanth Lagaave.

सहस बदन तुम्हरो यश गावे।

अस कहि श्रीपति कंठ लगावे।।

Glossary of Key Awadhi Words

1. Sahas : Thousand.

2. Badan : Faces or mouths.

3. Tumharo: Your, referring to Hanuman.

4. Yash : Glory or praise.

5. Gaave : Sing or extol.

6. Asa : Thus or in this manner.

7. Kahi : Said or spoke.

8. Shripati : Lord Vishnu or Lord Rama (husband of Goddess Lakshmi).

9. Kanth : Neck or embrace.

10. Lagaave : Embrace or hug.

Meaning of the Chaupai

"With thousands of mouths, your glory is sung, and so saying, Lord Rama embraced you."

Hidden Spiritual Secrets

1. Sahas Badan Tumharo Yash Gaave

- Infinite Praise for Infinite Virtues :

The phrase "thousands of mouths" signifies the countless virtues of Hanuman, which even the most eloquent beings find endless to describe. His qualities—devotion, strength, wisdom, and humility—are universally celebrated.

Hidden Wisdom :

Hanuman's boundless virtues symbolize the infinite potential within each individual. The more we align with divinity, the more our qualities are recognized and celebrated by the universe.

Practical Insight:

Focus on cultivating virtues like devotion, strength, and humility in your own life. These qualities naturally attract admiration and respect.

2. Asa Kahi Shripati Kanth Lagaave

- Divine Embrace as the Ultimate Reward:

Lord Rama's act of embracing Hanuman demonstrates the divine's immense love and gratitude for sincere service. This embrace is symbolic of spiritual unity and acknowledgment of the devotee's efforts.

Hidden Wisdom:

The embrace represents the merging of the individual soul (jivatma) with the supreme soul (paramatma). True devotion leads to oneness with the divine.

Practical Insight:

Seek spiritual connection through unwavering faith and selfless service. When your actions align with divine will, you experience an inner sense of unity and fulfillment.

Deeper Mystical Insights

1. Thousand Mouths as a Symbol of Eternity

The reference to "thousands of mouths" signifies the timeless nature of Hanuman's virtues. Just as the divine qualities of Hanuman are eternal, so too is the soul's potential for greatness.

2. Embrace as a Symbol of Moksha

Lord Rama's embrace signifies liberation (moksha), where the devotee is freed from the cycle of birth and death and merges with the divine.

3. Rama's Acknowledgment of Hanuman's Role

Hanuman's selfless dedication to serving Lord Rama is not only acknowledged but deeply valued. This teaches that even the divine cherishes acts of pure devotion.

Ramcharitmanas Connection

- Hanuman's Glory:

Throughout the Ramcharitmanas, Hanuman's qualities are described as unmatched, from his strength in battle to his intelligence and devotion. His glory is sung not only by mortals but also by divine beings.

- Divine Embrace:

The act of embracing Hanuman reflects the intimate relationship between Lord Rama and his devotees. It is a moment of ultimate grace and recognition.

Practical Application in Daily Life

1. Recognize Your Potential:

Like Hanuman, cultivate your virtues. Dedicate your strengths to the service of a higher purpose.

2. Seek Inner Unity:

Meditate on the divine qualities of devotion, selflessness, and humility. These qualities help you connect with the divine within yourself.

3. Celebrate the Good in Others:

Like the "thousands of mouths" praising Hanuman, take time to recognize and appreciate the virtues of those around you.

4. Offer Selfless Service:

Perform actions without expecting rewards. The divine acknowledgment, like Rama's embrace, comes naturally to those who serve selflessly.

Conclusion

This Chaupai glorifies Hanuman's unmatched virtues and reminds us that devotion and selfless service lead to divine recognition and spiritual unity. Lord Rama's embrace symbolizes the ultimate reward for a life dedicated to truth and righteousness.

Chaupai 14

Sankadik Brahmadi Munisa,

Narad Sarad Sahit Ahisa.

सनकादिक ब्रह्मादि मुनिसा।

नारद सारद सहित अहीसा।।

Glossary of Key Awadhi Words

1. Sankadik : Refers to the four Kumaras (Sanaka , Sanandana, Sanatana, and Sanatkumara), eternal sages known for their wisdom and detachment.

2. Brahmadi : Refers to Lord Brahma and other celestial beings.

3. Munisa : Great sages or ascetics.

4. Narad : Sage Narada, a divine messenger and devotee of Lord Vishnu.

5. Sarad : Goddess Saraswati, the goddess of knowledge and wisdom.

6. Sahit : Along with or accompanied by.

7. Ahisa : Lord Shesha, the cosmic serpent on which Lord Vishnu rests.

Meaning of the Chaupai

"The four Kumaras, Lord Brahma, sages, Narada, Saraswati, and Lord Shesha all sing your praises."

Hidden Spiritual Secrets

1. Universal Acknowledgment of Hanuman's Virtues

This verse emphasizes that beings across realms—celestial, intellectual, and spiritual—revere Hanuman. From the eternally wise Kumaras to the mighty Lord Brahma, all acknowledge his devotion, wisdom, and strength.

Hidden Wisdom :

Hanuman's virtues transcend worldly limitations. They are universal and timeless, resonating with both human and divine beings.

Practical Insight :

Cultivate qualities that inspire respect and admiration across diverse spheres of life, such as devotion, humility, and integrity.

2. Sankadik and Their Symbolism

The four Kumaras are symbols of pure knowledge and detachment. Their praise for Hanuman highlights his alignment with ultimate truth and spiritual wisdom.

Esoteric Insight :

Hanuman embodies the balance of action and detachment—serving with dedication while remaining free from ego and attachment.

Practical Insight :

Practice detachment while performing your duties. Focus on the action, not the outcome, to maintain peace and clarity.

3. Narada as a Devotee and Messenger

Narada, known for spreading devotion and wisdom, praises Hanuman as a role model of devotion to Lord Rama.

Hidden Wisdom:

Hanuman's devotion sets a benchmark for all seekers, illustrating how selfless service leads to divine acknowledgment.

Practical Insight :

Let devotion guide your actions. Whether through prayer, meditation, or service, remain connected to your higher purpose.

4. Saraswati and Ahisa

- **Saraswati's Praise:** The goddess of knowledge admires Hanuman for his wisdom and eloquence, as seen in his diplomatic and articulate interactions in the Ramayana.

- **Ahisa (Lord Shesha) :** The cosmic serpent, a symbol of divine support and balance, acknowledges Hanuman's role in upholding dharma.

Hidden Wisdom :

Even the sources of knowledge (Saraswati) and balance (Shesha) recognize Hanuman's exemplary qualities. This underscores the completeness of his character.

Practical Insight :

Seek wisdom (symbolized by Saraswati) and balance (symbolized by Shesha) in your endeavors. These qualities enhance your ability to serve effectively.

Deeper Mystical Insights

1. Praise from the Cosmos

The inclusion of celestial beings in Hanuman's praise signifies his cosmic relevance. His virtues are not confined to the mortal realm but resonate across the spiritual spectrum.

2. Hanuman as a Conduit of Divine Will

Hanuman's life reflects the divine will. His actions serve as a reminder that when we align with dharma, even the cosmos supports and celebrates us.

Ramcharitmanas Connection

- **Hanuman's Role as the Ideal Devotee :**

In the Ramcharitmanas, Hanuman's unwavering dedication to Lord Rama earns him praise from sages, gods, and celestial beings alike.

- **Universal Recognition :**

This Chaupai mirrors Hanuman's universal appeal and the admiration he garners from beings across realms.

Practical Application in Daily Life

1. Be Universally Admirable :

Emulate Hanuman's qualities—selflessness, wisdom, and devotion—to inspire respect and admiration from all.

2. Seek Balance and Wisdom :

Incorporate the principles of Saraswati (knowledge) and Ahisa (balance) in your life. This helps you navigate challenges with clarity and composure.

3. Align with Divine Will :

Like Hanuman, dedicate your actions to a higher purpose. When you align with truth and righteousness, you naturally attract support and acknowledgment.

Conclusion

This Chaupai highlights Hanuman's universal virtues, acknowledged by divine, celestial, and intellectual beings alike. It inspires us to cultivate qualities that transcend boundaries and align us with the cosmic order.

Chaupai 15

Jam Kuber Digpal Jahan Te,

Kavi Kovid Kahin Sake Kahan Te.

यम कुबेर दिग्पाल जहाँ ते।

कवि कोविद कहि सकें कहाँ ते।।

Glossary of Key Awadhi Words

1. Jam : Yama, the lord of death.

2. Kuber : Lord of wealth and treasures.

3. Digpal : Guardians of the directions; celestial protectors of the eight cardinal points.

4. Jahan Te : From where or to whom.

5. Kavi : Poets or those skilled in composing verses.

6. Kovid : Scholars, learned individuals, or intellectuals.

7. Kahin Sake : Can describe or articulate.

8. Kahan Te : From where or how.

Meaning of the Chaupai

"Even Yama (the lord of death), Kuber (lord of wealth), the Digpals (guardians of directions), and learned poets and scholars fail to describe your greatness. How can mere mortals attempt to comprehend it?"

Hidden Spiritual Secrets

1. Hanuman's Divine Glory Beyond Comprehension

This verse highlights Hanuman's divine virtues and infinite greatness, which surpass the understanding of even celestial beings like Yama, Kuber, and the Digpals.

Hidden Wisdom :

Hanuman's qualities, rooted in devotion, humility, and strength, are so profound that even the most powerful and learned beings cannot fully articulate them.

Practical Insight:

Greatness is often beyond words or titles. True virtue, like Hanuman's, is expressed through action, selflessness, and service.

2. Yama, Kuber, and Digpals as Symbolic Forces

- Yama represents mortality and justice, indicating that Hanuman's influence transcends even the natural laws of life and death.

- Kuber symbolizes material wealth, emphasizing that spiritual greatness outweighs material possessions.

- Digpals represent universal balance, underscoring Hanuman's role in maintaining cosmic harmony.

Hidden Wisdom:

Hanuman's greatness is not confined to material or mortal realms but spans the physical, metaphysical, and spiritual domains.

Practical Insight :

Seek balance in life, recognizing that spiritual growth transcends material success and worldly power.

3. The Limitations of Intellect

The Chaupai conveys that human intellect, no matter how refined (*Kavi* and *Kovid*), cannot grasp the infinite. Hanuman's essence is felt through faith, devotion, and spiritual experience rather than intellectual analysis.

Practical Insight :

Let go of the need to fully understand everything intellectually. Open your heart to faith, devotion, and the experiential aspect of spirituality.

Deeper Mystical Insights

1. Beyond Mortal Understanding

This Chaupai invites humility by reminding us of the finite nature of human understanding when confronted with the infinite divine.

2. Faith and Devotion Over Reason

Hanuman's greatness reflects the boundlessness of devotion and service, which surpasses logic and reason.

Ramcharitmanas Connection

- Divine Transcendence :

Tulsidas frequently emphasizes that divine qualities cannot be fully articulated. Here, he uses powerful celestial and intellectual beings to illustrate the point.

- Hanuman as a Universal Force:

Hanuman's role in the Ramayana extends beyond aiding Rama; he represents cosmic balance, devotion, and spiritual transcendence.

Practical Application in Daily Life

1. Embrace Humility :

Acknowledge the limits of your knowledge and intellect. True wisdom begins with humility.

2. Balance Material and Spiritual :

Like Kuber and Yama, worldly pursuits and responsibilities are important but must be balanced with spiritual growth.

3. Focus on Action :

Greatness is not defined by how much you are praised but by the selflessness and impact of your actions.

4. Trust the Divine :

Have faith in the unseen and embrace the mysteries of life with devotion and gratitude.

Conclusion

This Chaupai underscores Hanuman's boundless greatness, which transcends the comprehension of even the most powerful and learned beings. It inspires us to cultivate humility, devotion, and faith, recognizing that some truths are meant to be experienced rather than explained.

Chaupai 16

Tum Upkar Sugrivahi Kinha,

Ram Milaye Rajpad Dinha.

तुम उपकार सुग्रीवहिं कीन्हा।

राम मिलाय राजपद दीन्हा।।

Glossary of Key Awadhi Words

1. Tum : You; referring to Hanuman.

2. Upkar : Favor or benevolence.

3. Sugrivahi : To Sugriva, the exiled monkey king.

4. Kinha : Did or performed.

5. Ram : Lord Rama, the incarnation of Vishnu.

6. Milaye : United or brought together.

7. Rajpad : The royal throne or kingship.

8. Dinha : Gave or granted.

Meaning of the Chaupai

"You did a great favor to Sugriva by reuniting him with Lord Rama and helping him reclaim his royal throne."

Hidden Spiritual Secrets

1. Hanuman's Role as a Divine Facilitator

This Chaupai highlights Hanuman's selfless service in reuniting Sugriva with Lord Rama. Through his intervention, Sugriva not only regained his lost kingdom but also aligned himself with divine purpose.

Hidden Wisdom:

Hanuman acts as a bridge between the divine (Lord Rama) and those in need (Sugriva). Similarly, spiritual guides or mentors help individuals connect with their higher purpose.

Practical Insight:

Be a bridge of kindness and support for others. Use your abilities to uplift those who are struggling, just as Hanuman did.

2. Symbolism of Sugriva and the Throne

- Sugriva's Exile : Represents the human condition of feeling lost, disconnected, or in conflict.

- Hanuman's Intervention : Symbolizes the divine grace that helps resolve internal struggles.

- The Throne : Signifies self-mastery and alignment with one's true purpose.

Hidden Wisdom :

Reclaiming the "throne" is a metaphor for regaining control over one's life and destiny through divine support and self-realization.

Practical Insight :

When you feel disconnected or lost, seek guidance through prayer, mentorship, or introspection. True strength lies in accepting help when needed.

3. The Power of Connection

Hanuman's greatest strength lies in his ability to create meaningful connections. By introducing Sugriva to Rama, he facilitated a transformative relationship that benefited both Sugriva and the larger mission of Dharma.

Practical Insight:

Use your relationships and networks to create positive outcomes, fostering growth and harmony for everyone involved.

Deeper Mystical Insights

1. The Role of a Devotee

Hanuman epitomizes the ideal devotee, always acting selflessly for the benefit of others and the fulfillment of divine will.

2. Unity with the Divine

Sugriva's meeting with Rama symbolizes the moment of spiritual awakening, where the individual soul reconnects with the Supreme Soul.

Ramcharitmanas Connection

- Sugriva's Redemption :

In the Ramcharitmanas , Hanuman helps Sugriva overcome his fear of Vali (his brother) and regain his confidence. His actions not only restore Sugriva's throne but also strengthen the alliance for Rama's mission to rescue Sita.

- Hanuman as a Problem-Solver :

Hanuman's unwavering faith and resourcefulness make him an indispensable ally in resolving conflicts and achieving divine goals.

Practical Application in Daily Life

1. Be a Source of Help :

Like Hanuman, extend support to those who are in need. Even small acts of kindness can lead to transformative outcomes.

2. Facilitate Positive Connections :

Use your relationships and skills to bring people together for mutual benefit and shared purpose.

3. Seek and Offer Guidance :

When faced with challenges, don't hesitate to seek help from mentors or trusted friends. Similarly, offer your wisdom and assistance to others.

4. Reclaim Your Inner Strength :

Just as Sugriva reclaimed his throne, focus on regaining control over areas of your life where you feel powerless.

Conclusion

This Chaupai celebrates Hanuman's role as a selfless guide and problem-solver. It reminds us to uplift others through service and create meaningful connections that lead to shared success and spiritual growth.

Chaupai 17

Tumharo Mantra Vibhishan Mana,

Lankeshwar Bhaye Sab Jag Jana.

तुम्हरो मंत्र विभीषन माना।

लंकेश्वर भए सब जग जाना।।

Glossary of Key Awadhi Words

1. Tumharo : Your; referring to Hanuman.

2. Mantra : Advice, counsel, or guidance; often with spiritual or strategic significance.

3. Vibhishan : The brother of Ravana, known for his righteousness.

4. Mana : Accepted or followed.

5. Lankeshwar : King of Lanka, referring to Vibhishan.

6. Bhaye : Became or transformed into.

7. Sab : All or everyone.

8. Jag : The world or universe.

9. Jana : Knew or learned.

Meaning of the Chaupai

"Vibhishan heeded your counsel, and as a result, he became the King of Lanka, a fact known to the entire world."

Hidden Spiritual Secrets

1. Hanuman as a Spiritual Guide

Hanuman's advice to Vibhishan reflects his ability to inspire others to choose righteousness, even when faced with opposition or personal loss. Vibhishan's acceptance of Hanuman's counsel led to his transformation from an outcast to a king.

Hidden Wisdom :

True guidance doesn't merely address external challenges but also transforms the seeker internally, aligning them with Dharma (righteousness).

Practical Insight :

When offering advice, focus on inspiring others to act in alignment with their higher self and moral values, just as Hanuman did.

2. The Symbolism of Vibhishan's Transformation

- Vibhishan : Represents the soul seeking righteousness amidst the chaos of material desires and familial attachments.

- Hanuman's Counsel : Symbolizes divine wisdom that helps the soul make righteous choices.

- Kingship of Lanka : Signifies the reward of spiritual alignment—inner sovereignty and mastery over one's lower tendencies (Lanka as the material world).

Practical Insight:

Seek wisdom that aligns your actions with truth and virtue, even if it requires standing against popular or familial opinions.

3. The Importance of Righteous Counsel

Hanuman's mantra not only influenced Vibhishan but also set a precedent that righteous actions lead to eventual success and recognition, regardless of initial struggles.

Hidden Wisdom :

Spiritual advice carries transformative power when offered with clarity, purity, and selflessness.

Practical Insight :

Always weigh advice based on its alignment with your core values and long-term well-being.

Deeper Mystical Insights

1. Hanuman as a Catalyst for Change

Hanuman's role in Vibhishan's transformation exemplifies the role of divine forces in helping individuals overcome internal and external conflicts to fulfill their spiritual purpose.

2. Leadership Rooted in Righteousness

Vibhishan's rise to kingship underscores the idea that true leadership is bestowed upon those who uphold Dharma, even under immense pressure.

3. Lanka as the Mind

Lanka can be seen as a metaphor for the human mind, filled with desires and ego (represented by Ravana). Vibhishan's kingship reflects the moment when righteousness gains control over these tendencies.

Ramcharitmanas Connection

- Vibhishan's Dilemma:

In the Ramcharitmanas, Vibhishan faced the moral challenge of opposing his brother Ravana. Hanuman's counsel gave him the courage to align with Dharma, despite the consequences.

- **Divine Intervention :**

Hanuman's role emphasizes that divine grace often manifests through the right words or actions at the right time, guiding individuals toward their destiny.

Practical Application in Daily Life

1. Seek and Follow Righteous Counsel :

When faced with moral dilemmas, look for advice grounded in truth and integrity, even if it challenges your comfort zone.

2. Be a Source of Wisdom :

Offer guidance to others that helps them align with their higher purpose and values.

3. Embrace Courage in Difficult Choices :

Like Vibhishan, have the courage to act righteously, even if it means going against popular opinions or personal ties.

4. Aspire for Inner Sovereignty :

Strive to master your lower tendencies, symbolized by Vibhishan's rise as the King of Lanka, to lead a life of self-control and spiritual fulfillment.

Conclusion

This Chaupai highlights Hanuman's role as a wise guide who inspires transformative decisions. It teaches us the value of righteous counsel, the courage to act upon it, and the rewards of aligning with Dharma.

Chaupai 18

Jug Sahasra Jojan Par Bhanu,

Leelyo Taahi Madhur Phal Janu.

जुग सहस्त्र योजन पर भानु।

लील्यो ताहि मधुर फल जानु।।

Glossary of Key Awadhi Words

1. Jug : An age or epoch; often refers to a vast expanse of time.

2. Sahasra : Thousand.

3. Jojan : A unit of distance in ancient India, approximately 8-9 miles.

4. Par : Beyond or across.

5. Bhanu : The Sun.

6. Leelyo: Swallowed or consumed.

7. Taahi : That or it.

8. Madhur : Sweet.

9. Phal : Fruit.

10. Janu : As or like.

Meaning of the Chaupai

"Covering thousands of leagues, you leaped to the Sun and swallowed it, thinking it to be a sweet fruit."

Hidden Spiritual Secrets

1. Hanuman's Fearlessness and Innocence

This verse refers to Hanuman's childhood act of leaping toward the Sun, mistaking it for a fruit. It symbolizes his boundless energy, innocence, and fearlessness, unhindered by any sense of limitation.

Hidden Wisdom :

The Sun represents knowledge, enlightenment, and ultimate truth. Hanuman's leap reflects the soul's innate aspiration to attain divine wisdom and illumination, undeterred by challenges.

Practical Insight :

Approach life's challenges with innocence and determination, as they often lead to unexpected enlightenment.

2. The Vast Leap (Sahasra Jojan)

The distance to the Sun emphasizes the magnitude of Hanuman's leap, symbolizing his extraordinary strength and capability.

Hidden Wisdom :

The leap signifies transcending limitations—physical, mental, and spiritual—to reach higher states of consciousness.

Practical Insight :

Set ambitious goals and trust in your inner strength to achieve them. Your potential often exceeds your perceived boundaries.

The Sun as a Sweet Fruit

Hanuman's perception of the Sun as a sweet fruit demonstrates his playful and childlike perspective, viewing even the grandest of celestial bodies with simplicity and joy.

Hidden Wisdom :

The sweetness of the fruit represents the joy and fulfillment found in seeking divine wisdom. The Sun's light, often harsh, is seen as nourishing when approached with the right attitude.

Practical Insight :

Adopt a childlike curiosity and joy in exploring life's mysteries. Challenges often transform into opportunities when viewed with positivity.

Deeper Mystical Insights

1. Hanuman as the Seeker of Divine Knowledge

The Sun, a symbol of divine light, is both the source of life and a representation of higher knowledge. Hanuman's leap reflects the soul's yearning to merge with its source of origin and enlightenment.

2. Transcending Limitations

By leaping toward the Sun, Hanuman demonstrates that courage, coupled with purity, enables one to transcend limitations and attain what seems unattainable.

3. Balancing Strength and Humility

While Hanuman exhibits immense strength in leaping toward the Sun, his humility allows him to see it as a fruit, maintaining his connection to innocence and joy.

Ramcharitmanas Connection

- Hanuman's Childhood :

This event is recounted in scriptures as a display of Hanuman's divine nature even as a child, emphasizing his boundless energy and devotion.

- Divine Play (Leela):

Hanuman's leap is an example of divine play, teaching us that spiritual progress can be joyous and fearless.

Practical Application in Daily Life

1. Aim High :

Set ambitious goals, even those that seem far out of reach. Trust in your inner strength to overcome obstacles.

2. Maintain Joy in Pursuits :

Approach challenges with a sense of playfulness and joy, as Hanuman did with the Sun.

3. Seek Enlightenment :

Let the Sun be a reminder to pursue higher knowledge and spiritual growth with determination and curiosity.

4. Balance Strength with Innocence:

Use your abilities with humility and maintain a childlike wonder in all that you do.

Conclusion

This Chaupai highlights Hanuman's fearless pursuit of the ultimate (symbolized by the Sun) and his boundless energy. It inspires us to transcend limitations, embrace challenges joyfully, and strive for higher wisdom with determination and innocence.

Chaupai 19

Prabhu Mudrika Meli Mukha Maahi,
Jaladhi Langhi Gaye Acharaj Naahi.

प्रभु मुद्रिका मेलि मुख माही।

जलधि लांघि गए अचरज नाही।।

Glossary of Key Awadhi Words

1. **Prabhu**: Lord or Master; here, referring to Lord Rama.

2. **Mudrika**: Ring; in this context, Lord Rama's signet ring.

3. **Meli**: Placed or kept.

4. **Mukha**: Mouth.

5. **Maahi**: Inside or within.

6. **Jaladhi**: Ocean.

7. **Langhi**: Crossed or leaped over.
8. **Gaye**: Went or accomplished.
9. **Acharaj**: Astonishment or miracle.
10. **Naahi**: Not.

Meaning of the Chaupai

"Placing Lord Rama's ring in your mouth, you leaped across the ocean—this was no wonder for you."

Hidden Spiritual Secrets

1. The Ring as a Symbol of Divine Grace

The ring represents Lord Rama's trust and grace. By carrying it, Hanuman becomes an instrument of divine will, gaining extraordinary strength and confidence.

- **Hidden Wisdom:**
- The "Mudrika" (ring) symbolizes divine empowerment. With the Lord's blessings, the impossible becomes achievable.
- **Practical Insight:**
- Carry faith and trust in the divine as your guide. With divine support, challenges become surmountable.

2. Crossing the Ocean

The ocean represents life's vast challenges. Hanuman's fearless leap demonstrates how faith, devotion, and purpose can overcome any obstacle.

- **Hidden Wisdom:**

The ocean is also symbolic of the separation between the soul and the Supreme. Hanuman's leap represents the journey of a devotee toward unity with the divine.

- **Practical Insight:**

View obstacles as opportunities for growth. Faith and determination can help you cross any metaphorical "ocean."

3. Acharaj Naahi (No Astonishment)

For Hanuman, achieving the seemingly impossible is a natural expression of his devotion to Lord Rama. This highlights the transformative power of divine connection.

- **Hidden Wisdom:**

Devotion aligns the individual with the infinite power of the divine, making miracles appear effortless.

- **Practical Insight:**

Trust in your higher purpose and divine support. With faith, what seems miraculous to others can become a natural part of your journey.

Deeper Mystical Insights

1. **Mudrika as the Seed of Divine Will**

The ring signifies the divine mission entrusted to Hanuman. It empowers him with clarity, purpose, and unwavering resolve.

2. **The Ocean as a Metaphor for the Mind**

In Vedantic philosophy, the ocean often represents the turbulent mind. Hanuman's leap signifies the power of devotion to calm the mind and achieve clarity.

3. **Hanuman as the Embodiment of Devotion**

Hanuman's act exemplifies the traits of an ideal devotee: humility, courage, and absolute surrender to the divine will.

Ramcharitmanas Connection

- **The Mission to Lanka:**

Carrying Rama's ring, Hanuman undertakes the mission to locate Sita in Lanka, symbolizing a devotee's unwavering dedication to fulfilling the divine purpose.

- **Empowerment by the Divine:**

Lord Rama's trust in Hanuman highlights how the divine empowers devotees to achieve extraordinary deeds.

Practical Applications in Daily Life

1. **Carry Your Faith:**

Let faith be your "Mudrika" as you face life's challenges. Trust in your higher purpose to guide you.

2. **Face Challenges with Determination:**

Like Hanuman crossing the ocean, approach life's challenges with courage, knowing you are supported by a higher power.

3. **Align with Divine Will:**

Serve others selflessly and stay aligned with your spiritual path, drawing strength from your connection to the divine.

4. **Recognize Your Inner Potential:**

With faith, your potential expands beyond perceived limitations, enabling you to achieve the seemingly impossible.

Conclusion

This Chaupai celebrates Hanuman's unwavering devotion and extraordinary feats, emphasizing the power of faith and divine connection. It reminds us to carry faith like a sacred token, face challenges with courage, and trust in the guidance of a higher power.

Chaupai 20

Durgam Kaaj Jagat Ke Jete,

Sugam Anugrah Tumhare Tete.

दुर्गम काज जगत के जेते।

सुगम अनुग्रह तुम्हरे तेते॥

Glossary of Key Awadhi Words

1. Durgam : Difficult or impossible to achieve.

2. Kaaj : Task or work.

3. Jagat : The world or universe.

4. Ke : Of or related to.

5. Jete : All or as many.

6. Sugam : Easy or simple.

7. Anugrah : Grace or blessing.

8. Tumhare : Your or because of you.

9. Tete : Become.

Meaning of the Chaupai

All the difficult tasks in the world become easy with your grace.

Hidden Spiritual Secrets

1. The Power of Divine Grace

This Chaupai emphasizes that Hanuman's blessings can simplify even the most challenging endeavors. His grace transforms insurmountable problems into manageable solutions.

Hidden Wisdom :

Difficulties arise when we rely solely on our limited abilities. With divine grace, we access strength and wisdom beyond our comprehension.

Practical Insight :

Seek divine grace through devotion, prayer, and selfless service. Trust in the higher power to guide you through life's challenges.

2. The Nature of Challenges

Challenges are often a test of faith and resilience. Hanuman's role as a remover of obstacles highlights the transformative power of devotion and courage in overcoming adversity.

Hidden Wisdom:

"Durgam" tasks are not inherently insurmountable; they appear so when approached without clarity, courage, or faith. Hanuman's blessings bring these qualities to the forefront.

Practical Insight:

Approach every challenge with the belief that it can be overcome, especially when supported by faith and divine blessings.

3. Transforming the Impossible into the Possible

Hanuman's grace symbolizes the power of devotion to transcend limitations. His blessings align one's inner strength with divine will, making even the impossible achievable.

Hidden Wisdom :

"Sugam" does not imply the absence of effort but rather the removal of unnecessary resistance, allowing tasks to flow naturally toward resolution.

Practical Insight :

Take proactive steps with faith and dedication, trusting that divine grace will smooth your path.

Deeper Mystical Insights

1. The Illusion of Difficulty

From a spiritual perspective, challenges (Durgam Kaaj) often stem from illusions of separation, fear, and ego. Hanuman's blessings clear these illusions, revealing the simplicity of truth.

2. Hanuman as the Energy of Transformation

Hanuman embodies strength, wisdom, and devotion—qualities that can transform the most daunting obstacles into opportunities for growth.

3. Faith as the Key to Grace

Grace (Anugrah) flows where there is faith and surrender. Hanuman's blessings are most potent when one approaches him with humility and trust.

Ramcharitmanas Connection

- Sita's Rescue :

Hanuman's actions in locating Sita and burning Lanka demonstrate his ability to make the impossible possible through courage, devotion, and divine guidance.

- Vibhishan's Transformation :

Hanuman's wise counsel and unwavering faith led Vibhishan to align with righteousness, simplifying what seemed like an insurmountable moral dilemma.

Practical Application in Daily Life

1. Invoke Hanuman's Grace :

Recite this Chaupai when facing a difficult task. Trust in Hanuman's blessings to guide and support you.

2. Transform Challenges into Opportunities :

View obstacles as chances to grow in strength, faith, and resilience. Seek guidance from a higher power to overcome them.

3. Cultivate Faith and Surrender :

Let go of fear and ego. Approach challenges with humility and confidence in divine support.

4. Align Actions with Righteousness :

Ensure that your efforts are rooted in truth and integrity. Hanuman's grace flows more readily when one's actions align with dharma.

Conclusion

This Chaupai celebrates Hanuman's ability to simplify life's complexities and overcome challenges through divine grace. It inspires us to approach difficulties with faith, courage, and trust in the transformative power of devotion.

Chaupai 21

Ram Duare Tum Rakhvaare,

Hot Na Agya Bin Paisaare.

राम द्वारे तुम रखवारे।

होत न आज्ञा बिनु पैसारे।।

Glossary of Key Awadhi Words

1. Ram : Lord Rama, symbolizing the ultimate truth and divinity.

2. Duare : Door or gateway, representing access to divine blessings or liberation.

3. Tum : You; refers to Lord Hanuman.

4. Rakhvaare : Guard or protector.

5. Hot Na : Does not happen.

6. Agya : Permission or command.

7. Bin : Without.

8. Paisaare : To pass through or enter.

Meaning of the Chaupai

"You are the protector of Lord Rama's door; none can enter without your permission."

Hidden Spiritual Secrets

1. Hanuman as the Gatekeeper of Divine Grace

This Chaupai highlights Hanuman's crucial role as the gatekeeper to Rama's blessings and liberation. His approval and grace are essential for those seeking to connect with the divine.

Hidden Wisdom :

The "door" to Lord Rama symbolizes the gateway to spiritual truth and liberation (moksha). Hanuman, as the protector, ensures that only the deserving—those with devotion, humility, and sincerity—gain access.

Practical Insight :

Cultivate the qualities of devotion and selflessness to seek Hanuman's grace, which is essential for reaching higher spiritual states.

2. Permission as a Symbol of Worthiness

The requirement of Hanuman's "permission" underscores the importance of purification before approaching divinity. Hanuman, embodying unwavering devotion and humility, sets the standard for seekers.

Hidden Wisdom:

This permission is not about exclusivity but about readiness. Only those who reflect Hanuman's virtues of devotion, courage, and humility can approach the divine.

Practical Insight :

Self-purification through discipline, service, and meditation is key to gaining the inner readiness to approach the divine.

3. The Role of Devotion in Spiritual Progress

Hanuman's role as the gatekeeper signifies that unwavering devotion (bhakti) is the most direct path to divinity.

Hidden Wisdom :

While knowledge and rituals have their place, Hanuman reminds us that pure devotion is the ultimate key to Rama's door.

Practical Insight :

Focus on fostering a heartfelt connection with the divine through devotion, love, and service to others.

Deeper Mystical Insights

1. The Door as a Metaphor for the Inner Journey

The "door" to Lord Rama is not an external entity but the entrance to the divine within. Hanuman guards this inner sanctuary, allowing entry only to those ready to transcend ego and ignorance.

2. Hanuman as the Embodiment of Dharma

By guarding Rama's door, Hanuman ensures that only those aligned with dharma (righteousness) can access divine grace.

3. Spiritual Readiness

The concept of requiring "permission" reflects the need for inner alignment and readiness. Hanuman helps seekers cultivate this readiness through his teachings and blessings.

Ramcharitmanas Connection

- Hanuman's Devotion to Rama :

In the Ramcharitmanas , Hanuman exemplifies the highest form of devotion. His unwavering commitment to Rama makes him the ideal gatekeeper to divine grace.

- **Sita's Search :**

When searching for Sita, Hanuman's ability to overcome immense challenges demonstrates his role as a protector and guide for those seeking liberation.

Practical Application in Daily Life

1. Seek Hanuman's Grace :

Regularly invoke Hanuman through prayers or chants, such as the Hanuman Chalisa, to seek his blessings and guidance on your spiritual path.

2. Cultivate Readiness :

Engage in self-purification through devotion, humility, and service to others to align with divine qualities.

3. Align with Dharma :

Live a life rooted in truth, compassion, and selflessness, as these qualities resonate with Hanuman's essence.

4. Focus on Inner Transformation :

Understand that the "door" to Lord Rama is an inner gateway. Meditate and reflect to connect with the divine within yourself.

Conclusion

This Chaupai emphasizes Hanuman's vital role as the protector of the path to divinity. It reminds us to embody the qualities of devotion, humility, and righteousness to gain access to higher spiritual realms. By seeking Hanuman's blessings, we align ourselves with the divine grace of Lord Rama.

Chaupai 22

Sab Sukh Lahai Tumhari Sarna,

Tum Rakshak Kahu Ko Darna.

सब सुख लहै तुम्हारी शरणा।

तुम रक्षक काहू को डरना।।

Glossary of Key Awadhi Words

1. Sab : All; signifies completeness or entirety.

2. Sukh : Happiness, peace, or comfort.

3. Lahai : Attain or achieve.

4. Tumhari : Yours; refers to Hanuman.

5. Sarna : Shelter, refuge, or protection.

6. Tum : You; again, refers to Hanuman.

7. Rakshak : Protector or guardian.

8. Kahu : To anyone.

9. Darna : Fear or to be afraid.

Meaning of the Chaupai

"All happiness is attained by taking refuge in you; with you as the protector, there is no need to fear anyone."

Hidden Spiritual Secrets

1. Refuge in Hanuman Brings Absolute Peace

Taking refuge in Hanuman represents surrendering one's ego and relying on his divine strength and guidance. This Chaupai emphasizes that complete surrender to Hanuman leads to unparalleled happiness and inner peace.

Hidden Wisdom :

Hanuman is not just a protector from external dangers but also a guide who helps overcome internal struggles, such as fear, doubt, and negativity.

Practical Insight :

Whenever faced with challenges or fears, remember Hanuman's strength and seek his shelter through prayer or meditation.

2. The Protector Who Eliminates Fear

Hanuman is depicted as the ultimate guardian who shields devotees from harm and fear. Whether the threat is physical, emotional, or spiritual, Hanuman's protection is absolute.

Hidden Wisdom :

Fear arises from attachment and ignorance. Hanuman's grace removes these root causes, replacing them with courage and clarity.

Practical Insight :

Invoke Hanuman's name (Jai Hanuman) in moments of fear or uncertainty to draw upon his divine strength.

3. Happiness Through Devotion

The Chaupai suggests that true happiness is not material but spiritual. By taking shelter in Hanuman, one aligns with higher virtues, leading to lasting peace and joy.

Hidden Wisdom :

Hanuman symbolizes devotion, humility, and service. Aligning with these qualities brings contentment that transcends worldly pleasures.

Practical Insight :

Pursue spiritual practices, like reciting the Hanuman Chalisa, to cultivate inner happiness and resilience.

Deeper Mystical Insights

1. The Refuge as Inner Surrender

Taking refuge in Hanuman is a metaphor for surrendering the ego and aligning with divine will. This surrender dissolves fear and opens the path to spiritual liberation (moksha).

2. The Source of Fearlessness

Hanuman's protection extends beyond the physical realm. By eliminating ignorance and ego, he provides a deeper sense of fearlessness that comes from understanding one's divine nature.

3. Universal Happiness

The phrase "Sab Sukh Lahai" implies that Hanuman's blessings are universal, accessible to anyone who seeks his shelter with sincerity.

Ramcharitmanas Connection

- Hanuman as Saviour:

Throughout the Ramcharitmanas , Hanuman repeatedly acts as a protector—saving Lakshman with the Sanjeevani herb, assisting Rama in his quest for Sita, and protecting devotees from harm.

- **Fearless Devotion :**

Hanuman's unshakable devotion to Rama inspires courage and fearlessness in those who follow his example.

Practical Application in Daily Life

1. Seek Hanuman's Shelter:

Begin your day with a prayer or chant to Hanuman, seeking his blessings for courage, peace, and happiness.

2. Face Challenges Fearlessly :

Remember that with Hanuman's protection, you can face any challenge without fear.

3. Cultivate Devotion :

Embrace qualities like devotion, humility, and service, which align you with Hanuman's essence and bring lasting happiness.

4. Overcome Internal Struggles :

Use meditation and reflection to surrender your fears, doubts, and ego to Hanuman's divine guidance.

Conclusion

This Chaupai emphasizes Hanuman's role as the ultimate refuge and protector. By surrendering to him, devotees experience fearlessness and true happiness. It reminds us that Hanuman's blessings are not limited to protection but extend to spiritual awakening and liberation.

Chaupai 23

Apan Tej Samharo Aapai,

Teenon Lok Haank Te Kaanpai.

आपन तेज सम्हारो आपै।

तीनों लोक हांक ते कांपै।।

Glossary of Key Awadhi Words

1. Apan : Own; refers to self.

2. Tej : Radiance, power, or energy.

3. Samharo : Control or restrain.

4. Aapai : By oneself.

5. Teenon Lok : The three worlds (Swarga—heaven, Prithvi—earth, Patal—netherworld).

6. Haank : Roar, shout, or command.

7. Kaanpai : Tremble or shake.

Meaning of the Chaupai

"You control your own immense power, and with your mighty roar, the three worlds tremble."

Hidden Spiritual Secrets

1. Self-Control as Supreme Power

Hanuman's ability to restrain his boundless power reflects his mastery over himself. Despite being immensely powerful, he uses his strength only when necessary and for righteous purposes.

Hidden Wisdom :

True strength lies not in showcasing power but in knowing when and how to use it. Restraint and self-discipline are marks of a wise individual.

Practical Insight :

Practice self-restraint in moments of anger, temptation, or impatience. Channel your energy constructively, just as Hanuman does.

2. The Roar that Shakes the Cosmos

Hanuman's roar symbolizes his divine authority and presence. It also represents the power of divine truth, which disrupts ignorance and brings about transformation across all realms.

Hidden Wisdom :

The trembling of the three worlds signifies the cosmic impact of divine actions. Hanuman's roar is a reminder that truth and righteousness are forces that resonate universally.

Practical Insight :

Speak and act with integrity, letting your words and deeds carry the weight of truth and purpose.

3. The Trembling of the Three Worlds

The Teenon Lok—heaven, earth, and the netherworld—tremble at Hanuman's command, signifying his unparalleled strength and divine stature.

Hidden Wisdom :

The three worlds also represent the three dimensions within us:

1. Heaven (Swarga) : The mind, seeking wisdom and clarity.

2. Earth (Prithvi) : The body, requiring discipline and balance.

3. Netherworld (Patal) : The subconscious, often clouded by fears and desires.

Hanuman's roar symbolizes the awakening of inner strength that balances and aligns these dimensions.

Practical Insight:

Meditate on Hanuman to awaken inner courage and clarity, especially during times of self-doubt or fear.

Deeper Mystical Insights

1. Restraint as Divine Wisdom

Hanuman's restraint over his immense power reflects the principle of tapasya (self-discipline). It is through control of one's energy that divine potential is fully realized.

2. The Transformative Roar

Hanuman's roar represents the AUM vibration, also present in Ram naam—the primordial sound that brings balance and order to the universe. It resonates through the physical, mental, and spiritual planes, dispelling negativity and awakening truth.

3. Impact of Divine Presence

The trembling of the three worlds symbolizes the transformative impact of divine energy, reminding us that righteousness always prevails over chaos.

Ramcharitmanas Connection

- Hanuman's Controlled Power :

In the Ramcharitmanas, Hanuman repeatedly demonstrates his ability to control his immense strength. For instance, while crossing the ocean to reach Lanka, he assumes a small form to remain undetected but unleashes his full power when needed.

- Cosmic Impact of Devotion :

Hanuman's actions, fueled by devotion to Lord Rama, have a universal impact, shaking the very fabric of existence and inspiring awe among gods, demons, and mortals alike.

Practical Application in Daily Life

1. Practice Self-Discipline:

Cultivate self-control in your actions and emotions. Use your energy for constructive and righteous purposes.

2. Speak with Authority:

Let your words reflect truth and confidence, inspiring respect and positive change in others.

3. Meditate for Inner Strength :

Meditate on Hanuman's form or chant his name to awaken courage and resilience in challenging situations.

4. Balance the Three Dimensions:

Align your mind, body, and spirit by addressing fears, cultivating discipline, and seeking clarity through introspection and devotion.

Conclusion

This Chaupai emphasizes Hanuman's unmatched power, his self-discipline, and his cosmic influence. It inspires us to cultivate self-restraint, act with integrity, and awaken the divine strength within.

Chaupai 24

Bhut Pisach Nikat Nahin Aavai,

Mahavir Jab Naam Sunavai.

भूत पिशाच निकट नहीं आवै।

महावीर जब नाम सुनावै।।

Glossary of Key Awadhi Words

1. Bhut : Ghosts or spirits; symbolic of fears or negative energies.

2. Pisach : Demons; often represent inner vices or destructive forces.

3. Nikat : Near or close.

4. Aavai : To come or approach.

5. Mahavir : Another name for Hanuman, meaning "Great Hero."

6. Naam : Name; refers to chanting or remembering Hanuman's name.

7. Sunavai : To hear or listen.

Meaning of the Chaupai

"Ghosts and evil spirits cannot come near when the name of the mighty Mahavir (Hanuman) is heard."

Hidden Spiritual Secrets

1. Protection Against Negative Energies

This Chaupai conveys the protective power of Hanuman's name. Chanting or even hearing his name creates a spiritual shield, dispelling negative influences.

Hidden Wisdom :

Bhut and Pisach symbolize not only external dangers but also internal struggles such as fear, doubt, and harmful thoughts. Invoking Hanuman aligns the individual with divine strength and courage.

Practical Insight :

When overwhelmed by fear or negativity, chant or meditate on Hanuman's name to regain inner peace and strength.

2. Mahavir: The Great Hero Within

Hanuman's title, Mahavir, reminds us of the latent heroism within ourselves. His name acts as a catalyst, awakening this inner strength.

Hidden Wisdom :

The act of remembering (Naam Sunavai) connects us with Hanuman's divine qualities—courage, fearlessness, and resolve—helping us overcome inner and outer demons.

Practical Insight:

Reflect on Hanuman's attributes and embody them in your actions. Face challenges with bravery and faith.

3. The Transformative Power of Divine Name

The sound vibrations of Hanuman's name carry immense spiritual power, capable of transforming the atmosphere and dispelling negativity.

Hidden Wisdom :

This Chaupai alludes to the universal power of divine names (Naamsmaran). Repeating the name of Hanuman aligns the mind with higher vibrations, creating a protective aura.

Practical Insight :

In times of distress or uncertainty, repeat Hanuman's name like a mantra. Let its vibrations guide you toward clarity and strength.

Deeper Mystical Insights

1. Symbolism of Bhut and Pisach:

- Bhut (ghosts) represent lingering fears or unresolved emotions.

- Pisach (demons) symbolize harmful habits, destructive patterns, or external negativity.

Chanting Hanuman's name dispels these influences, illuminating the mind and soul.

2. Sound as a Purifier :

The Naam (name) of Hanuman is likened to a purifying force. In Vedic tradition, sound is a tool for transformation, capable of cleansing negative energies from the physical and spiritual realms.

3. Faith as the Ultimate Defense :

This Chaupai highlights the importance of faith. Believing in Hanuman's protective power is itself a shield against harm.

Ramcharitmanas Connection

- Hanuman's Role as Protector :

In the Ramcharitmanas , Hanuman safeguards Lord Rama's devotees from harm. He exemplifies fearlessness and loyalty, inspiring devotion and trust in his protective powers.

- **Hanuman's Victory Over Evil :**

Hanuman vanquishes demons like Akshay Kumar and burns Lanka, symbolizing his ability to eradicate evil and restore dharma.

Practical Application in Daily Life

1. Chant Hanuman's Name :

Regularly recite Jai Hanuman or the Hanuman Chalisa to create a positive and protective energy field around you.

2. Face Your Fears:

Invoke Hanuman's name when confronting fears or challenges. Remember his qualities of bravery and resilience.

3. Cleanse Your Space :

Chanting or playing Hanuman's praises in your home or workspace can help dispel negative energies and promote peace.

4. Develop Inner Strength :

Let Hanuman's name remind you of your inner courage and potential to overcome obstacles.

Conclusion

This Chaupai celebrates Hanuman as a divine protector who dispels all negativity and fear. It teaches us to rely on his name as a source of strength and to cultivate the same fearlessness in our own lives.

Chaupai 25

Nasei Rog Harai Sab Peera,

Japat Nirantar Hanumat Beera.

नासै रोग हरै सब पीरा।

जपत निरंतर हनुमत बीरा।।

Glossary of Key Awadhi Words

1. Nasei : To be destroyed or eliminated.

2. Rog : Diseases or ailments, both physical and mental.

3. Harai : To remove or alleviate.

4. Sab : All or every.

5. Peera : Pain or suffering.

6. Japat : Chanting or repeating.

7. Nirantar : Continuously, without interruption.

8. Hanumat Beera : Brave Hanuman; referring to his divine and courageous form.

Meaning of the Chaupai

"All diseases are destroyed, and suffering is alleviated by the continuous chanting of the brave Hanuman's name."

Hidden Spiritual Secrets

1. Healing Power of Devotion

This Chaupai emphasizes the healing potential of Hanuman's name. Physical ailments (rog) and emotional or spiritual suffering (peera) are removed by unwavering devotion to Hanuman.

Hidden Wisdom :

Rog and peera are not limited to physical illnesses. They also symbolize inner turmoil, such as anxiety, fear, or ignorance. By meditating on Hanuman, one connects to a divine energy that harmonizes mind, body, and soul.

Practical Insight :

In times of illness or suffering, chant Hanuman's name as a meditative practice to invite divine healing and strength.

2. Nirantar: The Importance of Continuous Practice

The term nirantar signifies persistence and consistency. Just as physical exercise strengthens the body over time, consistent chanting aligns the mind and soul with divine vibrations.

Hidden Wisdom :

Regular devotion creates a positive energy field that repels negativity and restores balance to one's being.

Practical Insight :

Dedicate a few moments daily to chant Hanuman's name or recite the Hanuman Chalisa, fostering inner resilience and peace.

3. Hanuman as a Source of Vital Energy

Hanuman is called Beera (the brave one), representing vitality and courage. His name acts as a channel for these divine attributes, reinvigorating the devotee both physically and mentally.

Hidden Wisdom:

Hanuman's energy is transformative, empowering individuals to overcome not only illness but also life's challenges with strength and determination.

Practical Insight :

Invoke Hanuman's name to awaken courage and vitality when faced with challenges, whether they are health-related or emotional.

Deeper Mystical Insights

1. Disease as a Metaphor :

In spiritual terms, diseases (rog) also symbolize karmic imbalances or ignorance. Chanting Hanuman's name burns these impurities, facilitating spiritual growth.

2. Power of Vibrations :

The sound vibrations of Hanuman's name carry healing energy. Chanting creates a resonant frequency that purifies the mind, strengthens the body, and uplifts the spirit.

3. Suffering as a Teacher :

Suffering (peera) often prompts individuals to turn inward and seek higher truths. Hanuman's name serves as a reminder of the divine support available during such times.

Ramcharitmanas Connection

- Hanuman's Role as Healer :

In the Ramcharitmanas, Hanuman brings the Sanjeevani herb to save Lakshman, symbolizing his power to heal and restore life.

- **Hanuman's Devotion as a Cure :**

Tulsidas highlights that unwavering devotion to Hanuman not only solves worldly problems but also leads to spiritual liberation.

Practical Application in Daily Life

1. Healing Chant :

Recite Hanuman's name or the Hanuman Chalisa to invoke healing energies during times of physical or emotional distress.

2. Consistency is Key :

Make chanting or meditating on Hanuman's name a regular practice to experience its transformative power over time.

3. Seek Divine Strength:

When overwhelmed by challenges, remember Hanuman's bravery and draw strength from his example.

4. Create a Positive Environment :

Play devotional music dedicated to Hanuman to cleanse the energy of your surroundings and promote healing.

Conclusion

This Chaupai highlights the transformative and healing power of Hanuman's name. It teaches us the importance of unwavering faith and consistency in devotion as a means to overcome suffering and align with divine energy.

Chaupai 26

Sankat Te Hanuman Chhudave,

Man Kram Bachan Dhyan Jo Lave.

संकट से हनुमान छुड़ावै।

मन क्रम बचन ध्यान जो लावै।।

Glossary of Key Awadhi Words

1. Sankat : Troubles, difficulties, or calamities.

2. Te : From.

3. Hanuman : The divine monkey god, symbol of devotion, strength, and protector of devotees.

4. Chhudave : To liberate or rescue.

5. Man : Mind; referring to thoughts and intentions.

6. Kram : Actions or deeds.

7. Bachan : Words or speech.

8. Dhyan : Meditation or focus.

9. Jo : Whoever or those who.

10. Lave : Bring, direct, or dedicate.

Meaning of the Chaupai

"Hanuman rescues from all troubles those who direct their thoughts, words, and actions towards him with sincere meditation."

Hidden Spiritual Secrets

1. Sankat: Troubles as Catalysts for Growth

Life's difficulties (sankat) are often spiritual tests or opportunities for growth. Hanuman's role is to guide and rescue devotees who are sincerely devoted to him.

Hidden Wisdom :

Troubles arise from a disconnection with the divine or misalignment of thought, speech, and action. By meditating on Hanuman, one realigns these aspects and attracts divine grace.

Practical Insight :

When faced with challenges, turn to Hanuman with complete faith. Reflect on how the obstacle may lead to personal or spiritual development.

2. Man, Kram, Bachan: The Threefold Devotion

True devotion requires alignment in:

- Man : Thoughts should be focused and pure, free from doubt or negativity.

- Kram : Actions should be righteous, reflecting devotion and sincerity.

- Bachan : Words should be truthful, uplifting, and aligned with spiritual principles.

Hidden Wisdom :

This alignment creates a powerful synergy that attracts Hanuman's grace, removing obstacles from the devotee's path.

Practical Insight :

Cultivate mindfulness in your thoughts, deeds, and words. Make them a reflection of your devotion to Hanuman and the divine.

3. Dhyan: The Power of Focus

Meditation (dhyan) on Hanuman invokes his strength, wisdom, and courage. This focus establishes a connection that not only alleviates troubles but also provides clarity and inner peace.

Hidden Wisdom :

Meditation on Hanuman transcends mere ritual; it is a transformative practice that aligns the devotee with divine energy.

Practical Insight :

Visualize Hanuman's form and qualities during meditation. Use his image as a source of inspiration and strength during difficult times.

Deeper Mystical Insights

1. Hanuman as the Liberator :

Hanuman's role as a savior is deeply symbolic. He represents the divine force that removes ignorance (agyana) and fear, the root causes of all troubles.

2. Sankat as Maya (Illusion) :

Many difficulties are a result of attachment to worldly illusions. Meditating on Hanuman helps transcend this illusion and recognize one's inner strength.

3. Transformative Power of Surrender :

Surrendering to Hanuman with unwavering faith invokes his blessings, turning even the most difficult situations into opportunities for liberation.

Ramcharitmanas Connection

- Hanuman's Role in the Ramayana :

Throughout the Ramayana, Hanuman removes obstacles and alleviates the suffering of those who place their faith in him, from rescuing Sita to bringing the Sanjeevani herb.

- Tulsidas's Emphasis on Faith:

Tulsidas portrays Hanuman as the ultimate refuge for devotees, emphasizing that unwavering faith in Hanuman can overcome even the gravest troubles.

Practical Application in Daily Life

1. Meditation on Hanuman :

Set aside time daily to meditate on Hanuman's qualities, envisioning him as your protector and guide.

2. Align Thought, Word, and Deed :

Regularly evaluate whether your thoughts, words, and actions reflect your spiritual intentions.

3. Hanuman Chalisa as a Remedy :

Recite the Hanuman Chalisa with devotion during times of trouble to invoke his blessings and courage.

4. Surrender to Divine Will :

Trust in Hanuman's guidance and believe that he will help you navigate any obstacle.

Conclusion

This Chaupai underscores Hanuman's role as the savior of devotees from troubles. It reminds us to maintain unwavering faith and alignment in our thoughts, actions, and words, trusting in Hanuman's divine protection and guidance.

Chaupai 27

Sab Par Ram Tapasvi Raja,

Tin Ke Kaaj Sakal Tum Saja.

सब पर राम तपस्वी राजा।

तिन के काज सकल तुम साजा।।

Glossary of Key Awadhi Words

1. Sab Par : Above all or superior to all.

2. Ram : Lord Rama, the ideal king and an incarnation of Lord Vishnu.

3. Tapasvi : One who practices austerities or penance, symbolizing self-discipline and spiritual focus.

4. Raja : King; referring to Lord Rama as the ruler of both worldly and spiritual realms.

5. Tin Ke : Their or his.

6. Kaaj : Tasks, responsibilities, or duties.

7. Sakal : All or complete.

8. Tum : You, referring to Hanuman.

9. Saja : To accomplish or fulfill.

Meaning of the Chaupai

"Lord Rama, the supreme ascetic and ruler, stands above all. It is you, Hanuman, who accomplishes all his tasks."

Hidden Spiritual Secrets

1. Ram as the Supreme Tapasvi

Lord Rama is not only a king but also a tapasvi, embodying self-discipline, righteousness, and spiritual perfection. His reign is a metaphor for the ultimate harmony between worldly duties and spiritual aspirations.

Hidden Wisdom :

Rama's identity as a tapasvi shows that true leadership requires self-mastery and humility.

Practical Insight :

Follow Rama's example by balancing your responsibilities with spiritual growth. Let discipline and righteousness guide your actions.

2. Hanuman as the Divine Instrument

Hanuman is the ideal devotee, entrusted with carrying out Rama's divine will. His unwavering devotion and boundless energy make him the perfect executor of Rama's plans.

Hidden Wisdom:

Hanuman's role teaches that true service requires surrendering the ego and dedicating oneself to a higher purpose.

Practical Insight :

In your endeavors, align your efforts with a noble cause or higher purpose. Dedicate your actions to service and humility.

3. Collaboration Between the Divine and the Devotee

This Chaupai highlights the symbiotic relationship between the divine (Rama) and the devotee (Hanuman). While Rama is the source of divine will, Hanuman manifests that will through his actions.

Hidden Wisdom :

Divine grace and human effort work together to fulfill great purposes.

Practical Insight :

Trust in divine guidance but also take initiative and action. Success comes from the harmony of grace and effort.

Deeper Mystical Insights

1. Rama as the Supreme Consciousness :

Rama symbolizes the divine consciousness that governs the universe. Hanuman, as his devotee, represents the awakened energy (shakti) that brings the divine plan into action.

2. Hanuman's Devotion as the Key :

Hanuman's unquestioning faith and dedication to Rama demonstrate that selfless devotion transforms ordinary beings into divine instruments.

3. apas (Austerity) as a Path to Mastery:

Rama's identity as a tapasvi reminds us that self-discipline and sacrifice are essential for both worldly success and spiritual realization.

Ramcharitmanas Connection

- Hanuman's Role in Rama's Mission :

From finding Sita to building the bridge to Lanka and fighting Ravana, Hanuman plays a crucial role in executing Rama's plans. His actions reflect complete surrender to Rama's will.

- **Tulsidas's Devotion:**

Through this Chaupai, Tulsidas emphasizes Hanuman's unique position as both a servant and an integral part of Rama's divine mission.

Practical Application in Daily Life

1. Embrace Discipline :

Follow Rama's example by cultivating self-discipline and righteousness in your daily life.

2. Serve a Higher Purpose :

Like Hanuman, dedicate your actions to a noble cause. Recognize that your efforts can contribute to a greater good.

3. Trust in Divine Guidance:

Balance your efforts with faith in the divine. Trust that, like Rama's tasks, your duties are part of a larger plan.

4. Develop Devotion and Humility :

Emulate Hanuman's humility and devotion by serving others selflessly and aligning your actions with spiritual values.

Conclusion

This Chaupai celebrates Lord Rama's supreme authority and Hanuman's unparalleled devotion. It serves as a reminder to balance discipline and humility, align your actions with a higher purpose, and trust in divine guidance.

Chaupai 28

Aur Manorath Jo Koi Laave,

Soi Amit Jeevan Phal Paave.

और मनोरथ जो कोई लावे।

सोई अमित जीवन फल पावे।। ।

Glossary of Key Awadhi Words

1. Aur : Any other or additional.

2. Manorath : Desire, wish, or aspiration.

3. Jo Koi : Whoever or anyone.

4. Laave : Brings or places (symbolically presenting a wish to Hanuman).

5. Soi : That same or the specific one.

6. Amit : Infinite, immeasurable, or boundless.

7. Jeevan : Life or existence.

8. Phal : Fruit or reward.

9. Paave : Receives or attains.

Meaning of the Chaupai

"Whoever brings their heartfelt desires to Hanuman, they are granted infinite rewards and fulfillment in life."

Hidden Spiritual Secrets

1. Power of Faith in Hanuman

This Chaupai underscores Hanuman's benevolence and his role as the granter of wishes. When devotees approach Hanuman with sincerity and faith, their desires align with divine will, and they receive blessings beyond measure.

Hidden Wisdom :

Faith acts as the bridge between aspiration and fulfillment. Hanuman symbolizes divine intervention that removes obstacles and leads to success.

Practical Insight :

Offer your aspirations to Hanuman with complete trust. His grace can help you overcome challenges and achieve your goals.

2. Infinite Rewards (Amit Jeevan Phal)

The phrase Amit Jeevan Phal reflects not only material rewards but also spiritual growth and inner peace. Devotees gain contentment, strength, and a sense of purpose.

Hidden Wisdom :

True rewards lie in the transformation of the seeker. Hanuman's blessings guide devotees toward their highest potential.

Practical Insight :

Recognize that spiritual fulfillment often surpasses worldly desires. Seek Hanuman's grace not just for material gains but for inner peace and self-realization.

3. Alignment with Divine Will

When wishes are offered with purity and devotion, they align with the cosmic plan. Hanuman, as the executor of Lord Rama's will, ensures that only those desires beneficial to the devotee's spiritual progress are fulfilled.

Hidden Wisdom :

Desires rooted in selflessness and righteousness are more likely to bear fruit.

Practical Insight :

Reflect on your aspirations to ensure they align with higher values and contribute to your growth and the well-being of others.

Deeper Mystical Insights

1. Hanuman as a Wish-fulfiller :

Hanuman represents the energy that transforms desires into reality. His blessings are boundless, ensuring both worldly success and spiritual progress.

2. Purification of Desires :

Through devotion to Hanuman, desires are purified, leading to a deeper connection with divine consciousness.

3. The Symbolism of Offering Wishes :

Presenting wishes to Hanuman symbolizes surrendering ego-driven aspirations and trusting divine wisdom to guide outcomes.

Ramcharitmanas Connection

- Hanuman's Role as a Protector :

Throughout the Ramayana, Hanuman fulfills the wishes of those devoted to Lord Rama, whether it's Sugriva reclaiming his kingdom, Sita receiving hope, or Rama defeating Ravana.

- Tulsidas's Faith :

In composing the Hanuman Chalisa, Tulsidas demonstrates his own faith in Hanuman as the ultimate wish-fulfiller, inspiring devotees to approach him with trust and devotion.

Practical Application in Daily Life

1. Approach Hanuman with Sincerity :

Offer your wishes through prayer, recognizing Hanuman's role as a guide and protector.

2. Reflect on Your Aspirations:

Ensure your desires align with ethical and spiritual values. Avoid selfish or harmful intentions.

3. Cultivate Gratitude:

Celebrate the blessings you receive, whether they fulfill your wishes directly or lead to unexpected growth and wisdom.

4. Trust the Divine Timing :

Recognize that not all wishes are granted immediately or in the way you expect. Trust Hanuman's wisdom in fulfilling them appropriately.

Conclusion

This Chaupai assures devotees that Hanuman listens to their heartfelt desires and fulfills them in a way that brings infinite blessings. It emphasizes the power of faith, the importance of selfless aspirations, and the boundless rewards of devotion to Hanuman.

Chaupai 29

Charo Jug Pratap Tumhara,

Hai Parsiddha Jagat Ujiyara.

चारो युग प्रताप तुम्हारा।

है प्रसिद्ध जगत उजियारा।।

Glossary of Key Awadhi Words

1. Charo : All four.

2. Jug : Yugas, the four epochs in Hindu cosmology (Satya Yuga , Treta Yuga, Dvapara Yuga, and Kali Yuga).

3. Pratap : Glory, power, or influence.

4. Tumhara : Yours, referring to Hanuman.

5. Hai : Is or exists.

6. Parsiddha : Famous, well-known, or celebrated.

7. Jagat : World or universe.

8. Ujiyara : Light or illumination, symbolizing wisdom, knowledge, and truth.

Meaning of the Chaupai

"Your glory shines through all four ages and is renowned for illuminating the world."

Hidden Spiritual Secrets

1. Hanuman's Eternal Influence

This Chaupai emphasizes Hanuman's timeless relevance and universal glory. Across the four Yugas, his virtues, deeds, and devotion to Lord Rama remain a guiding light for humanity.

Hidden Wisdom :

Hanuman transcends the boundaries of time, symbolizing eternal truth and divine power. His presence assures devotees of guidance and support regardless of the age or circumstances.

Practical Insight :

Seek inspiration in Hanuman's qualities—devotion, strength, and humility—as timeless virtues that can lead you through life's challenges.

2. Illumination of the World (Jagat Ujiyara)

Hanuman's glory brings light to the world, dispelling darkness and ignorance. His actions serve as a beacon for those seeking knowledge, courage, and spiritual wisdom.

Hidden Wisdom :

The "light" of Hanuman represents not only external illumination but also the awakening of inner consciousness. It is the light that clears doubts, fears, and delusions.

Practical Insight :

Invoke Hanuman to illuminate your path in times of uncertainty, enabling you to act with clarity and confidence.

3. The Four Yugas as States of Being

The reference to the four Yugas can also symbolize stages in an individual's spiritual journey:

1. Satya Yuga (Truth) : The state of purity and enlightenment.

2. Treta Yuga (Righteousness) : The phase of moral striving.

3. Dvapara Yuga (Duality) : The struggle between good and evil within.

4. Kali Yuga (Darkness) : The state of ignorance and delusion.

Hidden Wisdom :

Hanuman's light shines equally in all these stages, guiding devotees toward spiritual progress regardless of where they stand.

Practical Insight :

Understand that Hanuman's presence is constant and unwavering, available to all who seek him sincerely.

Deeper Mystical Insights

1. Hanuman's Universal Nature :

Hanuman is not limited to a specific era, religion, or region. His virtues are universal, resonating with seekers of truth across all traditions.

2. Dispeller of Darkness :

Just as the rising sun dispels night, Hanuman's glory eradicates ignorance and instills wisdom. His influence helps devotees find purpose and direction.

3. Symbol of Hope in Kali Yuga :

In the current age of Kali Yuga, Hanuman is often invoked as a protector and guide. His name and stories serve as reminders of resilience and divine support.

Ramcharitmanas Connection

- Hanuman's Timeless Role :

In Ramcharitmanas, Tulsidas highlights Hanuman's unchanging devotion and strength across various episodes, reinforcing his eternal relevance.

- Illumination Through Bhakti (Devotion) :

Hanuman's life exemplifies how devotion to Lord Rama brings enlightenment and peace, irrespective of the age or era.

Practical Application in Daily Life

1. Invoke Hanuman's Guidance Daily :

Chant his name or meditate on his qualities to draw courage and clarity into your life.

2. Illuminate Your Inner World :

Let Hanuman's glory inspire you to dispel ignorance and cultivate wisdom in your thoughts and actions.

3. Embody Timeless Virtues :

Strive to practice devotion, humility, and strength—values that transcend time and uplift humanity.

4. Spread Light to Others :

Like Hanuman, be a source of hope and positivity for those around you.

Conclusion

This Chaupai highlights Hanuman's enduring influence and his role as an eternal source of illumination. It reassures devotees that his glory is not confined to a specific era but continues to guide and inspire across all times.

Chaupai 30

Sadhu Sant Ke Tum Rakhwaare,

Asur Nikandan Ram Dulaare.

साधु संत के तुम रखवारे।

असुर निकंदन राम दुलारे।।

Glossary of Key Awadhi Words

1. Sadhu : A holy person, ascetic, or saint dedicated to spiritual practices.

2. Sant : A saintly person, often referring to those devoted to God.

3. Ke : Of or for.

4. Tum : You, referring to Hanuman.

5. Rakhwaare : Protector or guardian.

6. Asur : Demons, representing negativity or evil forces.

7. Nikandan : Destroyer or vanquisher.

8. Ram : Lord Rama, the Supreme Divine.

9. Dulaare : Beloved or dear one.

Meaning of the Chaupai

"You are the protector of saints and sages, the destroyer of demons, and the beloved of Lord Rama."

Hidden Spiritual Secrets

1. Protector of the Righteous (Sadhu Sant Ke Rakhwaare)

Hanuman stands as a guardian for those who dedicate themselves to truth, spirituality, and righteousness. He ensures their safety, both physically and spiritually.

Hidden Wisdom :

Sadhu and Sant represent not only ascetics but also individuals striving for spiritual growth. Hanuman's role as their protector underscores his commitment to supporting purity and devotion in the world.

Practical Insight :

If you lead a life of righteousness and devotion, trust in Hanuman's guidance and protection against external and internal challenges.

2. Destroyer of Negativity (Asur Nikandan)

Demons (Asuras) symbolize the forces of ignorance, ego, and evil that disrupt the spiritual journey. Hanuman, as the destroyer of these forces, aids in overcoming obstacles.

Hidden Wisdom :

Hanuman's ability to vanquish demons mirrors the triumph of light over darkness and good over evil. His presence inspires inner strength and courage to face life's adversities.

Practical Insight :

When overwhelmed by negative emotions or challenges, call upon Hanuman to dispel them and restore clarity and balance.

3. The Beloved of Lord Rama (Ram Dulaare)

Hanuman's unwavering devotion makes him Lord Rama's dearest devotee. This highlights that pure, selfless love and service are the keys to divine grace.

Hidden Wisdom :

Hanuman's relationship with Lord Rama teaches the value of humility, loyalty, and surrender in the pursuit of spiritual progress.

Practical Insight :

Cultivate unconditional devotion in your relationships—with the Divine and with others—emphasizing service over self-interest.

Deeper Mystical Insights

1. Dual Role of Protection and Destruction :

Hanuman embodies both nurturing protection for the righteous and fierce destruction for negativity. This duality symbolizes balance—compassion combined with the strength to uphold justice.

2. Sadhu and Sant as States of Mind :

The Sadhu and Sant can also represent the tranquil and enlightened aspects of the mind. Hanuman protects these qualities from being overshadowed by negative tendencies.

3. Personal Transformation :

The Asuras within us are our fears, doubts, and harmful desires. Hanuman's grace enables us to conquer these and grow spiritually.

Ramcharitmanas Connection

- Hanuman's Devotion to Rama :

In the Ramcharitmanas , Hanuman's selfless love for Lord Rama defines his identity as *Ram Dulaare. His every action reflects his dedication to Rama's mission.

- **Defender of the Saints :**

Hanuman is often depicted aiding sages and devotees in distress, reinforcing his role as their eternal protector.

Practical Application in Daily Life

1. Seek Protection in Devotion :

Pray to Hanuman for safety and guidance, especially when pursuing spiritual or moral goals.

2. Overcome Inner Demons :

Reflect on Hanuman's strength to inspire courage in overcoming personal challenges or destructive habits.

3. Serve with Devotion :

Emulate Hanuman's example by offering service selflessly, whether to a higher power or your community.

4. Balance Compassion and Strength :

Strive to protect the vulnerable while standing firm against injustice or negativity.

Conclusion

This Chaupai highlights Hanuman's dual role as the guardian of righteousness and the destroyer of evil. It emphasizes his unparalleled devotion to Lord Rama and his unwavering support for those who walk the path of virtue.

Chaupai 31

Ashta Siddhi Nau Nidhi Ke Daata,

Asvar Din Janki Mata.

अष्ट सिद्धि नौ निधि के दाता।

असवर दिन जानकी माता।।

Glossary of Key Awadhi Words

1. Ashta Siddhi : The eight supernatural powers as described in ancient scriptures.

2. Nau Nidhi : The nine treasures or forms of wealth mentioned in Hindu mythology.

3. Ke : Of or belonging to.

4. Daata : Giver or bestower.

5. Asvar : Blessing or boon.

6. Din : Given or granted.

7. Janki : Another name for Sita, consort of Lord Rama.

8. Mata : Mother, referring to Sita here with reverence.

Meaning of the Chaupai

"You are the bestower of the eight supernatural powers and the nine treasures, a boon granted to you by Mother Janki (Sita)."

Hidden Spiritual Secrets

1. Ashta Siddhi (The Eight Powers)

The eight supernatural powers are:

1. Anima : The ability to shrink in size.

2. Mahima : The ability to expand to an immense size.

3. Garima : The ability to become extremely heavy.

4. Laghima : The ability to become extremely light.

5. Prapti : The ability to acquire anything desired.

6. Prakamya : The ability to fulfill desires.

7. Ishatva : The ability to have divine powers of creation.

8. Vashitva : The ability to control all.

Hidden Wisdom :

These powers represent mastery over the self and the elements, achieved through intense devotion and purity of mind. Hanuman's possession of these powers demonstrates his divine nature and total surrender to Lord Rama.

Practical Insight:

True power lies in self-mastery and the ability to use one's capabilities for the greater good.

2. Nau Nidhi (The Nine Treasures)

The nine treasures are believed to include forms of wealth, prosperity, and abundance. These treasures are symbolic of material and spiritual fulfillment.

Hidden Wisdom :

Hanuman's ability to bestow these treasures signifies his role as a divine benefactor. Those who revere him are granted not only material blessings but also spiritual wisdom.

Practical Insight :

Seek balance between material prosperity and spiritual growth, knowing that true wealth includes peace, contentment, and devotion.

3. Blessings of Janki Mata

Sita, as an embodiment of purity and divine grace, bestowed these powers upon Hanuman as a reward for his unwavering devotion and service.

Hidden Wisdom :

The blessings of Janki Mata highlight the importance of surrender and humility in devotion. Hanuman's greatness stems not from seeking power but from his selfless love and service to Rama and Sita.

Practical Insight :

Approach life with humility and devotion; blessings will naturally flow as a result of your sincerity.

Deeper Mystical Insights

1. Powers as Symbols of Inner Strength

The Ashta Siddhis and Nau Nidhis are not just supernatural phenomena but representations of inner potential unlocked through devotion, discipline, and grace.

2. Role of Divine Feminine

Janki Mata, as the bestower of these blessings, represents the nurturing and empowering aspect of divinity. Her grace is essential for spiritual growth and prosperity.

3. Hanuman's Selflessness

Despite possessing immense powers, Hanuman remains humble, using his gifts solely in service of Lord Rama. This underscores the ideal use of power—for the benefit of others.

Ramcharitmanas Connection

- Hanuman's Devotion to Sita :

In the Ramcharitmanas, Hanuman's meeting with Sita in Lanka is a turning point. His reverence and devotion earn him her blessings, making him a conduit of divine grace.

- Symbol of Divine Grace :

Sita's blessings signify that devotion leads to divine grace, which can empower a devotee with unimaginable abilities.

Practical Application in Daily Life

1. Use Your Talents for Service :

Like Hanuman, use your strengths and abilities for the welfare of others.

2. Seek Balance in Life :

Strive for material success, but ensure it is aligned with spiritual principles and ethical living.

3. Value Grace Over Power :

Recognize that true power comes through humility and divine blessings, not through force or ego.

4. Revere the Divine Feminine :

Respect and honor the nurturing aspects of life, symbolized by Janki Mata.

Conclusion

This Chaupai illustrates Hanuman's divine status as the bestower of blessings, a grace earned through his unparalleled devotion. It serves as a reminder that true greatness lies in selfless service, humility, and the blessings of divine grace.

Chaupai 32

Ram Rasayan Tumhare Pasa,

Sada Raho Raghupati Ke Dasa.

राम रसायण तुम्हरे पासा।

सदा रहो रघुपति के दासा।।

Glossary of Key Awadhi Words

1. Ram : Lord Rama, the Supreme Being in human form.

2. Rasayan : Elixir or essence; something that rejuvenates and nourishes.

3. Tumhare : Yours or in your possession.

4. Pasa : With or near you.

5. Sada : Always or forever.

6. Raho : Remain or stay.

7. Raghupati : Another name for Lord Rama, meaning the Lord of the Raghu dynasty.

8. Ke : Of or belonging to.

9. Dasa : Servant or devotee.

Meaning of the Chaupai

"You possess the elixir of devotion to Lord Rama, and you remain forever His devoted servant."

Hidden Spiritual Secrets

1. Ram Rasayan (The Elixir of Devotion)

The term "Ram Rasayan" refers to the essence of devotion and the spiritual bliss derived from unwavering love and surrender to Lord Rama.

Hidden Wisdom :

This "elixir" is symbolic of immortality in spiritual terms—freedom from the cycle of birth and death (moksha). Hanuman's devotion to Rama is so profound that it acts as a divine remedy for all sorrows and struggles.

Practical Insight :

Meditate on the qualities of Lord Rama—truth, compassion, and righteousness—to cultivate inner peace and spiritual strength.

2. Eternal Devotion (Sada Raho Raghupati Ke Dasa)

Hanuman exemplifies the ideal devotee who remains steadfast in his service to Lord Rama. His humility and dedication are unwavering, even in the face of immense challenges.

Hidden Wisdom :

True devotion transcends rituals and is rooted in constant remembrance of the Divine. Being a "dasa" (servant) is not servitude but a state of surrender and divine connection.

Practical Insight :

Approach your daily duties as acts of devotion. By aligning your actions with a higher purpose, you can transform ordinary tasks into spiritual practice.

Deeper Mystical Insights

1. Ram Rasayan as Inner Transformation

The elixir of devotion purifies the mind and heart, removing ego, desires, and ignorance. Hanuman, as its possessor, symbolizes the power of devotion to heal and transform the seeker.

2. Service as a Path to Liberation

Hanuman's role as a devoted servant illustrates that selfless service is a direct path to spiritual liberation. Service to the Divine and others leads to the dissolution of the ego and unity with the higher Self.

3. Possession of the Divine Essence

Hanuman does not seek worldly treasures but cherishes the "Ram Rasayan"—a metaphor for eternal bliss. This highlights the supremacy of spiritual wealth over material possessions.

Ramcharitmanas Connection

Hanuman's Role as Rama's Servant :

In the Ramcharitmanas, Hanuman constantly serves Lord Rama, whether by carrying His messages, retrieving the Sanjeevani herb, or fighting in battles. This unwavering devotion is his true "elixir."

- Devotion as the Ultimate Goal :

The text emphasizes that devotion (*bhakti*) is the easiest and most fulfilling path to spiritual realization. Hanuman personifies this teaching.

Practical Application in Daily Life

1. Focus on the Divine Essence :

Keep your thoughts centered on higher values and ideals, just as Hanuman keeps the essence of Lord Rama close to his heart.

2. Serve Others Selflessly :

Use your talents and energy to serve others without expecting rewards. This will bring you closer to the Divine.

3. Seek Inner Bliss :

Instead of chasing external pleasures, focus on cultivating inner peace through devotion, meditation, and self-reflection.

4. Be Humble and Dedicated :

Like Hanuman, always remain humble, no matter how much you achieve. Dedicate your efforts to a higher cause.

Conclusion

This Chaupai reminds us that true wealth lies in devotion and service. By keeping the "Ram Rasayan" close to our hearts and following Hanuman's example of humility and dedication, we can navigate life's challenges with grace and find eternal bliss.

Chaupai 33

Tumre Bhajan Ram Ko Paave,

Janam Janam Ke Dukh Bisraave.

तुमरे भजन राम को पावे।

जनम जनम के दुख बिसरावे।।

Glossary of Key Awadhi Words

1. Tumre : Your.

2. Bhajan : Devotional song or worship.

3. Ram : Lord Rama, the Supreme Being in human form.

4. Ko : To or for.

5. Paave : Attain or reach.

6. Janam Janam : Lifetimes or repeated births.

7. Ke : Of or belonging to.

8. Dukh : Sorrow, suffering, or pain.

9. Bisraave : Forget or be relieved of.

Meaning of the Chaupai

"By singing your praises and devotion, one attains Lord Rama and forgets the sorrows of countless lifetimes."

Hidden Spiritual Secrets

1. Bhajan as a Path to Liberation

The act of singing Hanuman's praises or meditating on his qualities is described as a gateway to Lord Rama, the ultimate goal of devotion. Hanuman represents unwavering devotion, and by aligning with his energy, the seeker naturally draws closer to the Divine.

Hidden Wisdom :

Devotional practice is not just about recitation but about cultivating a heartfelt connection with the Divine. This connection has the power to dissolve accumulated sorrows from countless lifetimes.

Practical Insight :

Engage in regular devotional activities like chanting, prayer, or reflection to deepen your bond with the Divine.

2. Relief from Lifetimes of Suffering

The Chaupai highlights the concept of karmic cycles—how past actions influence the present and future. Devotion to

Hanuman and Lord Rama acts as a purifying force that frees the devotee from these cycles of sorrow.

Hidden Wisdom :

This liberation is not just an escape but a transformation of perspective. Devotion aligns the individual with divine grace, which helps transcend suffering.

Practical Insight :

When facing challenges, focus on your devotional practice to cultivate resilience and find peace amidst adversity.

Deeper Mystical Insights

1. Bhajan as the Essence of Spiritual Practice

Devotional singing (Bhajan) is not merely an act of worship; it harmonizes the mind, body, and soul. It raises one's vibrations and connects the seeker with the universal consciousness.

2. Attaining Rama Through Hanuman

Hanuman's praises serve as a medium to reach Lord Rama. This highlights Hanuman's role as a bridge between the devotee and the Divine. His selfless devotion becomes a guiding light for others.

3. Forgetting Sorrows of Many Lifetimes

The phrase "Janam Janam Ke Dukh" suggests the burden of karmic impressions. Bhajan is a way to dissolve these impressions, allowing the seeker to experience spiritual freedom and bliss.

Ramcharitmanas Connection

- Hanuman as the Eternal Devotee :

In the Ramcharitmanas , Hanuman is depicted as an ideal devotee whose life revolves around Lord Rama. By praising Hanuman, devotees align themselves with his energy and devotion.

- Transcending Sorrow :

Lord Rama's grace, often facilitated by Hanuman, is shown to relieve even the deepest sorrows, as seen in the lives of Sugriva, Vibhishana, and others.

Practical Application in Daily Life

1. Practice Daily Bhajan :

Set aside time to sing or chant devotional songs. This practice calms the mind and brings clarity and joy.

2. Focus on Positivity :

Let devotion guide your thoughts and actions. When faced with negativity or sorrow, redirect your energy to your spiritual practice.

3. Seek Divine Connection :

Use Hanuman as an inspiration for unwavering devotion and service. His qualities can help you strengthen your connection to the Divine.

4. Release Past Sorrows:

Understand that devotion has the power to dissolve not just immediate troubles but the deeper patterns of suffering rooted in past lifetimes.

Conclusion

This Chaupai encapsulates the transformative power of devotion. By engaging in Hanuman's Bhajan, one draws closer to Lord Rama, experiences divine grace, and transcends the sorrows of countless lifetimes.

Chaupai 34

Anta Kaal Raghubar Pur Jayi,

Jahan Janma Hari Bhakta Kahayi.

अंत काल रघुबर पुर जाई।

जहाँ जन्म हरी भक्त कहाई।।

Glossary of Key Awadhi Words

1. Anta Kaal : End of life, or the final moments before death.

2. Raghubar : Lord Rama, the best of the Raghu dynasty.

3. Pur : Abode or city, referring to the divine realm of Lord Rama.

4. Jayi : To go or reach.

5. Jahan : Where.

6. Janma : Birth or reincarnation.

7. Hari : Another name for Lord Vishnu or Rama, meaning one who removes suffering.

8. Bhakta : Devotee or worshipper.

9. Kahayi : Called or known as.

Meaning of the Chaupai

"In the final moments of life, the devotee who worships Hanuman is taken to the divine abode of Lord Rama, and wherever they are reborn, they are known as a devotee of Hari (Lord Rama)."

Hidden Spiritual Secrets

1. Attaining the Divine Abode

The Chaupai suggests that unwavering devotion to Hanuman ensures liberation from the cycle of birth and death. The soul of such a devotee ascends to Raghubar Pur, the spiritual realm of Lord Rama.

Hidden Wisdom :

This journey represents spiritual liberation (moksha), achieved through grace and devotion. The devotee's unwavering focus on the Divine at the time of death guarantees eternal union with Rama.

Practical Insight :

Live a life of devotion and righteousness so that your mind remains connected to the Divine, even in your final moments.

2. Rebirth as a Devotee

The second part emphasizes that even if the devotee is reborn, they will continue to carry their devotion and connection to Lord Rama, demonstrating the eternal bond between the devotee and the Divine.

Hidden Wisdom :

This suggests that spiritual progress is never lost. Devotion to Hanuman and Rama creates an eternal imprint on the soul.

Practical Insight :

Engage in consistent spiritual practices, knowing that the fruits of devotion will carry forward beyond this lifetime.

Deeper Mystical Insights

1. Anta Kaal as a Test of Devotion

The mind's focus at the moment of death determines the soul's destination. A lifetime of devotion ensures that the devotee's thoughts are absorbed in Lord Rama during their final moments.

2. Hanuman as a Guide to Rama's Abode

Hanuman is seen as the gatekeeper and facilitator of access to Lord Rama's divine realm. His blessings help devotees achieve liberation and maintain their connection to the Divine across lifetimes.

3. Devotion Transcends Death

The Chaupai highlights the power of devotion to transcend the impermanence of life and death. It assures devotees that their connection to Rama, facilitated by Hanuman, is eternal.

Ramcharitmanas Connection

- **Hanuman's Role as a Savior :**

In the Ramcharitmanas , Hanuman rescues many devotees from peril, guiding them to safety and divine grace. This Chaupai reflects his role in guiding devotees not just in life but also after death.

- **Eternal Devotion :**

Tulsidas himself prays for eternal devotion to Rama, irrespective of his births. This aligns with the assurance given in this Chaupai.

Practical Application in Daily Life

1. Prepare for Anta Kaal :

- Cultivate a mindset of devotion and mindfulness.

- Regularly recite the name of Rama and meditate on his qualities to ensure your thoughts remain centered on him.

2. Strengthen Your Connection with Hanuman :

- Seek Hanuman's blessings for guidance in life and beyond.

- Chant Hanuman Chalisa as a daily practice to stay aligned with divine grace.

3. Embrace the Eternal Nature of Devotion :

- Recognize that devotion is timeless and will accompany you across lifetimes.

- Focus on spiritual progress without fear of setbacks.

4. Live a Righteous Life :

- Align your actions with Dharma to prepare your soul for its divine journey.

Conclusion

This Chaupai assures devotees that their devotion to Hanuman and Rama guarantees spiritual liberation or a rebirth as a devotee. It emphasizes the eternal bond between the devotee and the Divine, transcending the limitations of life and death.

Chaupai 35

Aur Devta Chitta Na Dharai,

Hanumat Sei Sarva Sukh Karai.

और देवता चित्त न धरै।

हनुमत सेई सर्व सुख करै।।

Glossary of Key Awadhi Words

1. Aur : Other or another.

2. Devta : Deity or divine being.

3. Chitta : Mind or attention.

4. Na Dharai : Does not place or focus.

5. Hanumat : Refers to Hanuman, the devoted servant of Lord Rama.

6. Sei : He (Hanuman).

7. Sarva : All or complete.

8. Sukh : Joy, happiness, or peace.

9. Karai : Grants or provides.

Meaning of the Chaupai

"Do not focus your mind on other deities; Hanuman alone provides all happiness and fulfillment."

Hidden Spiritual Secrets

1. Single-Minded Devotion

This Chaupai emphasizes exclusive devotion to Hanuman, symbolizing the power of focused worship. It teaches that channeling one's energy toward a single divine being magnifies spiritual and material benefits.

Hidden Wisdom :

Hanuman, as the ideal devotee of Lord Rama, represents the pinnacle of faith and surrender. Worshipping him strengthens the devotee's connection to Rama and ensures blessings in all areas of life.

Practical Insight :

Avoid scattering your spiritual energy by worshipping multiple deities without focus. Choose a path or deity that resonates deeply with your heart.

2. Hanuman as the Embodiment of Service

Hanuman's selfless devotion to Lord Rama makes him a symbol of divine grace. Devotion to Hanuman aligns the devotee with the virtues of humility, service, and strength.

Hidden Wisdom :

Hanuman not only grants material happiness but also leads the devotee toward spiritual liberation by connecting them to Lord Rama.

Practical Insight :

Practice selfless service (seva) in your daily life to invoke Hanuman's blessings and experience fulfillment.

Deeper Mystical Insights

1. Hanuman as the Gateway to Lord Rama

Hanuman is often seen as the intermediary between the devotee and Lord Rama. Worshipping Hanuman ensures direct access to Rama's grace, as Hanuman embodies Rama's infinite compassion and power.

2. Exclusive Devotion Simplifies Spiritual Practice

The Chaupai discourages unnecessary complexity in worship by suggesting that devotion to Hanuman alone is sufficient for attaining all forms of happiness. This reflects the idea that simplicity and focus are key to spiritual success.

3. Material and Spiritual Fulfillment

Hanuman's blessings encompass both worldly joy and spiritual growth, making him a holistic guide for devotees.

Ramcharitmanas Connection

- Hanuman as the Ideal Devotee :

In the Ramcharitmanas , Hanuman's unwavering loyalty to Lord Rama makes him the epitome of devotion. This Chaupai echoes the sentiment that focusing on such a devotee grants all blessings.

- Grace Through Simplicity :

The Ramcharitmanas often emphasizes single-minded devotion over ritualistic worship of multiple deities. This Chaupai aligns with Tulsidas's overall message of simplicity in devotion.

Practical Application in Daily Life

1. Simplify Your Worship :

- Focus your devotion on Hanuman as a representation of selfless service and divine strength.

- Recite the Hanuman Chalisa regularly to deepen your connection.

2. Emulate Hanuman's Virtues :

- Practice humility, loyalty, and dedication in your relationships and responsibilities.

- Seek to serve others selflessly, as Hanuman served Lord Rama.

3. Align with a Higher Purpose :

- Let Hanuman inspire you to channel your energy toward meaningful pursuits, both spiritual and material.

4. Cultivate Inner Peace :

- Trust that devotion to Hanuman will bring you the joy and fulfillment you seek, reducing anxiety about worldly concerns.

Conclusion

This Chaupai teaches the power of exclusive devotion to Hanuman, who serves as a divine conduit to Lord Rama. By focusing your mind on Hanuman, you can experience both worldly happiness and spiritual peace.

Chaupai 36

Sankat Katei, Mitein Sab Peera,

Jo Sumire Hanumat Balbira.

संकट कटे मिटे सब पीरा।

जो सुमिरे हनुमत बलबीरा।।

Glossary of Key Awadhi Words

1. Sankat : Crisis, difficulty, or trouble.

2. Katei : Get cut, removed, or resolved.

3. Mitein : Erased, diminished, or removed.

4. Sab : All.

5. Peera : Pain or suffering.

6. Sumire : Remember, meditate, or think upon.

7. Hanumat : Referring to Hanuman, the powerful and devoted servant of Lord Rama.

8. Balbira : Mighty or powerful, an epithet of Hanuman.

Meaning of the Chaupai

"All crises and suffering are resolved when one remembers Hanuman, the mighty and powerful servant of Lord Rama."

Hidden Spiritual Secrets

1. Hanuman as the Protector in Times of Crisis

This Chaupai reveals Hanuman's role as a divine protector who resolves all difficulties faced by the devotee. By meditating on Hanuman, one invokes his strength, courage, and divine power to overcome life's struggles.

Hidden Wisdom :

The phrase "Sankat Katei" indicates that Hanuman's divine intervention in times of distress removes suffering and obstacles, restoring peace and balance.

Practical Insight :

In times of personal turmoil or hardship, remember Hanuman's strength. Through faith and devotion, challenges are transformed into opportunities for growth and strength.

2. The Power of Remembrance (Sumire)

The verse emphasizes the power of remembering Hanuman in times of crisis. This act of remembrance (Sumire) is not just a mental exercise, but a spiritual practice that aligns the devotee with divine energy, helping them to overcome difficulties.

Hidden Wisdom :

Devotion and remembrance are powerful tools. By focusing on the divine, the devotee invokes spiritual power that can dissipate pain and suffering.

Practical Insight :

In moments of despair or fear, invoke the name of Hanuman with full faith. This remembrance becomes a conduit for divine grace, which dispels negativity and sorrow.

3. Mighty Strength (Balbira)

Hanuman's title, Balbira, highlights his unmatched strength, both physically and spiritually. This line reinforces the idea that Hanuman, in his infinite power, can eliminate all forms of suffering when called upon with devotion.

Hidden Wisdom :

The might of Hanuman transcends the physical realm. His strength is not just in his physical prowess but in his unwavering devotion to Lord Rama, which grants him cosmic power.

Practical Insight :

Draw upon the inner strength that comes from your connection to the divine. No challenge is insurmountable when one has faith and devotion as their strength.

Deeper Mystical Insights

1. The Nature of Suffering (Sankat)

In spiritual terms, suffering is often seen as an opportunity for transformation. This Chaupai suggests that remembrance of Hanuman serves as a reminder that all suffering is temporary and can be overcome with faith.

Esoteric Insight:

Suffering (Sankat) is often a result of disconnection from the divine. By turning to Hanuman in times of distress, one realigns with the divine presence, which offers the strength to transcend pain.

2. The Healing Power of Devotion

The act of remembering Hanuman (Sumire) becomes a healing practice. When the devotee surrenders to the divine, they activate an innate power that neutralizes all obstacles and suffering.

Esoteric Insight :

The power of remembrance, when accompanied by true devotion, becomes a healing force. Hanuman, as the embodiment of devotion, serves as the channel through which the devotee connects to divine healing energy.

Ramcharitmanas Connection

- Hanuman as the Divine Savior:

In the Ramcharitmanas , Hanuman's unwavering devotion to Lord Rama allows him to perform miraculous feats, such as bringing the Sanjeevani herb to heal Lakshmana. His ability to alleviate suffering is a consistent theme.

- The Role of Faith :

This verse reinforces the importance of faith in Hanuman. His power to alleviate suffering is not only through his divine attributes but also through the unwavering faith of the devotee in his ability to help.

Practical Application in Daily Life

1. Invoke Divine Protection in Times of Trouble :

Whenever you face challenges or suffering, take a moment to remember Hanuman with faith. His power will support you in overcoming obstacles.

2. Cultivate Remembrance as a Practice :

Make the practice of remembering Hanuman part of your daily routine. Whether through chanting, prayer, or meditation, remembrance serves as a spiritual anchor.

3. Strengthen Your Connection to the Divine :

By turning to Hanuman in times of crisis, you strengthen your inner resilience and faith. Know that no difficulty is too great for the divine power to handle.

Conclusion

This Chaupai is a powerful reminder of Hanuman's role as a protector who removes suffering and resolves all crises. It encourages us to remember him with unwavering faith, recognizing that the path to overcoming obstacles is through devotion, strength, and the power of divine remembrance.

Chaupai 37

Jai Jai Jai Hanuman Gosain,

Kripa Karahu Gurudev Ki Naai.

जय जय जय हनुमान गोसाईं।

कृपा करहु गुरुदेव की नाईं।।

Glossary of Key Awadhi Words

1. Jai Jai Jai : Victory, praise, or triumph, repeated to emphasize reverence.

2. Hanuman : The revered deity, known for his strength, wisdom, and devotion.

3. Gosain : Lord or master, a title denoting respect and reverence, here referring to Lord Hanuman.

4. Kripa : Grace, mercy, or divine blessing.

5. Karahu : Do, bestow, or grant.

6. Gurudev : Spiritual teacher, divine guide, or the revered figure who provides wisdom and protection.

7. Naai : The word used here signifies a variant of "Naath," meaning Lord or protector.

Meaning of the Chaupai

"Victory, victory, victory to Lord Hanuman, the revered Gosain! Please bestow your grace, O Gurudev, the protector of all."

Hidden Spiritual Secrets

1. The Power of Repeated Praise (Jai Jai Jai)

The repetition of "Jai Jai Jai" in this Chaupai signifies the strength of devotion and praise. Chanting or reciting the divine name three times amplifies the energy and blessings, invoking a profound sense of divine presence and protection.

Hidden Wisdom :

Repetition of divine names or praises is a powerful spiritual tool. The more we engage in devotional chanting, the more our hearts and minds align with the divine will, inviting strength and protection into our lives.

Practical Insight :

Regular chanting or recitation of sacred words can be a simple but effective practice to bring peace and divine protection into your life. It helps quiet the mind and deepen your connection with the divine.

2. Hanuman as the Divine Master (Gosain)

By calling Hanuman "Gosain," this Chaupai emphasizes his role as the supreme divine master, the one to whom all devotees turn for strength and guidance. He is not just a protector but also a teacher, guiding souls to the path of devotion and righteousness.

Hidden Wisdom:

Hanuman, as "Gosain," embodies the qualities of divine leadership: protection, guidance, and unshakeable devotion to Lord Rama. His role is to lead us on the path of spiritual growth and service.

Practical Insight :

Invoke Hanuman's guidance in your own spiritual journey. Surrender your obstacles to him, trust in his protection, and follow his example of selfless service and unwavering faith.

3. The Call for Divine Grace (Kripa)

"Kripa Karahu" is a humble request for divine grace. It highlights the understanding that only through the grace of a higher power can the devotee overcome life's challenges. Hanuman's grace is an unshakable force that empowers devotees to transcend worldly limitations.

Hidden Wisdom :

Grace, or "Kripa," is the divine intervention that empowers the devotee to succeed where human strength fails. It is through grace that even the most insurmountable obstacles become manageable.

Practical Insight :

Seek divine grace in times of difficulty. Recognize that not everything is within your control, and by surrendering to the divine, you open the door to support and blessings that guide you through challenges.

Deeper Mystical Insights

1. Divine Blessings Through Humility

This Chaupai reminds us that humility is the key to receiving grace. Hanuman's role as a divine servant teaches us that surrendering to the higher will and seeking grace with a humble heart allows us to receive the greatest spiritual benefits.

Esoteric Insight :

In spiritual terms, humility is the gateway to divine blessings. The more we humble ourselves, the more we allow divine energy to flow freely into our lives, removing obstacles and bestowing peace.

2. Hanuman as the Divine Protector and Guide

As "Gosain" and "Naai," Hanuman represents both the protector and the guide. He is the embodiment of divine strength, wisdom, and devotion. Through his grace, the devotee can achieve anything, no matter how impossible it may seem.

Esoteric Insight :

Hanuman's dual role as protector and guide reflects the ideal relationship between the devotee and the divine. We are meant to be both protected and taught by the divine to walk a righteous path.

Ramcharitmanas Connection

- Divine Empowerment Through Faith :

In the Ramcharitmanas, Hanuman's devotion to Lord Rama is unparalleled. This Chaupai mirrors that same unwavering devotion, calling upon Hanuman's grace to empower the devotee on their spiritual journey.

- Hanuman as the Ideal Devotee :

The Chaupai underscores Hanuman's perfect devotion and his selfless service to Lord Rama. As the perfect devotee, Hanuman exemplifies the qualities of humility, strength, and devotion that every follower should aspire to.

Practical Application in Daily Life

1. Invoke Divine Protection :

Whenever you face adversity, remember to invoke Hanuman's protection through prayer, chanting, or affirmations. His divine energy can help you overcome any obstacle.

2. Cultivate Humility :

Approach life with humility, recognizing that your strength and success come from the divine. Surrender to the higher will and trust that you will be guided through challenges.

3. Seek Divine Grace :

Understand that divine grace is not earned but is given freely to those who are open to it. Be receptive and humble in your prayers, and trust that grace will flow into your life.

4. Align Yourself with Divine Purpose :

Just as Hanuman serves Lord Rama with complete dedication, aim to align yourself with a higher purpose. Let your actions reflect your devotion and commitment to the greater good.

Conclusion

This Chaupai encapsulates the essence of divine devotion, grace, and protection. By praising Hanuman as both the master and the protector, it reminds us of the power of humility and surrender in the face of life's challenges. It is through divine grace that all obstacles are overcome, and with faith, we can achieve the seemingly impossible.

Chaupai 38

Jo Shat Baar Path Kare Koi,

Chhuti Bandhai, Maha Sukh Hoi.

जो सत बार पाठ करै कोई।

छूटहि बंदि महा सुख होई।।

Glossary of Key Awadhi Words

1. Jo : Whoever.

2. Shat Baar : A hundred times.

3. Path : Recitation, or the act of reading or chanting.

4. Kare Koi : Anyone who does.

5. Chhuti : Release, freedom, or liberation.

6. Bandhai : Bonds, ties, or attachments.

7. Maha Sukh : Great happiness or supreme joy.

8. Hoi : Will be or will receive.

Meaning of the Chaupai

"Whoever recites this path a hundred times will be freed from all bonds and will attain supreme happiness."

Hidden Spiritual Secrets

1. The Power of a Hundred Recitations (Shat Baar Path)

Reciting this path a hundred times signifies an intense and focused spiritual practice. Repetition is not only a ritual but a means to connect deeply with the divine energy. The act of repeating the sacred words so many times transforms the individual spiritually, making them more receptive to divine guidance and blessings.

Hidden Wisdom :

The hundred recitations represent a concentrated effort to connect with the divine will. The number hundred is often used to symbolize completeness, or the manifestation of a deep spiritual connection. This practice brings clarity of mind and purifies the heart.

Practical Insight :

Use repetition as a tool to deepen your connection to the divine. Chanting a sacred name or prayer multiple times can be a powerful way to focus the mind and invite divine energy into your life.

2. Freedom from Bonds (Chhuti Bandhai)

The "bonds" refer to the attachments that keep the individual bound to the material world—whether it be the attachment to desires, material wealth, relationships, or past experiences. Chanting with devotion and sincerity loosens these bonds and facilitates a release from worldly distractions.

Hidden Wisdom :

Chanting not only liberates one from external attachments but also frees the mind from internal limitations. These mental and emotional "bonds" often prevent spiritual progress, but with regular practice, one can experience freedom from these ties.

Practical Insight :

Identify the areas in your life where you feel tied down by attachment—whether to material things or unhealthy patterns of thought. Use prayer or mantra chanting as a way to detach from these limitations, cultivating spiritual freedom.

3. The Promise of Supreme Happiness (Maha Sukh Hoi)

The "Maha Sukh" is not merely fleeting pleasure but the ultimate peace and happiness that comes from aligning with the divine. It refers to an inner joy that transcends external circumstances, one that comes from spiritual fulfillment and liberation.

Hidden Wisdom :

True happiness arises when the soul is in harmony with the divine. It is a state of bliss that is independent of external conditions. This Chaupai reminds us that through devotion and spiritual practice, one can attain this supreme joy, regardless of external circumstances.

Practical Insight :

Seek happiness from within. By cultivating practices such as prayer, meditation, and mantra chanting, you can find lasting peace and joy that is not affected by the chaos of the outer world.

Deeper Mystical Insights

1. The Number Hundred as Spiritual Completion

The number hundred signifies spiritual completeness and mastery. It represents a complete offering of oneself to the divine, an effort that goes beyond superficial devotion. In this context, the repetition of a hundred recitations symbolizes the devotee's dedication and commitment to the divine path.

Esoteric Insight :

The number one hundred is symbolic of the entire spiritual journey—one that spans both the outer and inner realms of existence. It is the culmination of dedication, perseverance, and faith.

2. Repetition as a Means of Transformation

Chanting a sacred verse repeatedly creates a transformative shift within the individual. It is not just an external act, but a process of purifying the mind, body, and soul. With each recitation, the individual sheds layers of ignorance, leading to a deeper understanding and experience of spiritual peace.

Esoteric Insight :

Repetition, when performed with devotion, becomes a spiritual alchemy. It turns the ordinary act of chanting into a powerful tool for personal and spiritual transformation, leading to freedom from the distractions and illusions of the material world.

Ramcharitmanas Connection

- Hanuman's Devotion :

In the Ramcharitmanas , Hanuman's unwavering devotion to Lord Rama is exemplified through his consistent acts of service. His total surrender to Lord Rama's will and his dedication to performing his duties without expectation of reward are central to his character. The repetition of prayers or chants, as Hanuman did, strengthens one's relationship with the divine and purifies the heart.

- The Power of the Divine Name :

The power of repeating Lord Rama's name or Hanuman's name is a recurring theme in the Ramcharitmanas . It is through the constant chanting of the divine name that the devotee experiences liberation and supreme joy.

Practical Application in Daily Life

1. Incorporate Regular Recitation :

Commit to a regular practice of reciting sacred texts, prayers, or mantras. Whether it's reciting Hanuman's name or other divine mantras, repetition can help you stay centered and spiritually aligned.

2. Free Yourself from Attachments :

Identify and release attachments that are holding you back. Through consistent spiritual practice, such as prayer or chanting, you can loosen these ties and move toward spiritual freedom.

3. Seek Inner Fulfillment :

True happiness is found within. Use spiritual practices to cultivate a state of peace, harmony, and joy that is independent of external circumstances.

4. Dedicate Yourself to the Divine:

Offer your time, energy, and efforts to the divine through devotion. Through sustained dedication and perseverance, you will experience spiritual growth and fulfillment.

Conclusion

This Chaupai emphasizes the transformative power of devotion, the act of reciting sacred prayers a hundred times as a means of liberation, and the promise of supreme happiness. By engaging in sincere and consistent spiritual practices, such as chanting, one can transcend attachments and experience profound inner peace and joy.

Chaupai 39

Joi Yeh Pade Hanuman Chalisa,

Hoye Siddhi Sakin Gaurisa.

जो यह पढ़े हनुमान चालीसा।

होय सिद्धि साखी गौरीसा।।

Glossary of Key Awadhi Words:

1. Joi: Whoever.
2. Yeh: This.
3. Pade: Recites or reads.
4. Hanuman Chalisa: The hymn of Hanuman comprising forty verses.
5. Hoye: Happens or attains.
6. Siddhi: Spiritual perfection or divine powers.

7. Sakhi: Witness.
8. Gaurisa: Lord of Gauri (another name for Lord Shiva).

Meaning of the Chaupai

Whoever reads the Hanuman Chalisa will attain success and reside in the presence of Lord Shiva, the source of all power and auspiciousness."

Hidden Spiritual Secrets

1. Union of Hanuman and Shiva

This verse subtly underscores the divine connection between Lord Hanuman and Lord Shiva. In Hindu tradition, Hanuman is often considered to be the Eleventh avatar of Lord Shiva, and his strength and power are derived from this connection. Reciting the Hanuman Chalisa, therefore, not only invokes the blessings of Hanuman but also draws upon the divine energy of Lord Shiva.

Hidden Wisdom :

By reciting the Hanuman Chalisa, a devotee is aligned with the cosmic energy of both Hanuman and Shiva, receiving the blessings of both deities, leading to spiritual success and divine protection.

Practical Insight :

Through devotion to Hanuman, one can tap into the infinite power of Shiva. As you recite the Chalisa, feel yourself connected to this divine source, opening yourself to spiritual success and guidance.

2. Siddhi as Spiritual Fulfillment

The term "Siddhi" in this context refers to the ultimate state of spiritual fulfillment, enlightenment, and accomplishment. It suggests that through the recitation of the Hanuman Chalisa, the devotee not only receives worldly success but also spiritual growth, inner peace, and harmony.

Hidden Wisdom :

Siddhi is not just success in material endeavors but signifies the attainment of self-realization, wisdom, and spiritual liberation. This verse reminds us that true success transcends the physical world and is rooted in the divine connection.

Practical Insight :

Seek success that aligns with your spiritual growth. Focus not only on material goals but also on cultivating inner peace, wisdom, and connection to the divine.

3. The Role of Lord Shiva (Gaurisa)

By invoking Lord Shiva as the ultimate source of power and auspiciousness, this verse emphasizes that true spiritual strength comes from the divine and is shared by the supreme force. Shiva, the destroyer of evil and the lord of transformation, represents both destruction and creation—two necessary components of spiritual growth.

Hidden Wisdom :

Shiva's power is not just in creation and destruction but in transformation—helping devotees shed their ego and limiting beliefs, ultimately leading them to enlightenment.

Practical Insight :

Trust in the transformative power of the divine. Let go of your fears and limitations, knowing that through devotion and surrender, the divine will guide you toward growth and spiritual awakening.

Deeper Mystical Insights

1. Integration of Divine Powers

This Chaupai highlights the integration of two powerful divine energies: that of Hanuman (devotion, courage, strength) and Shiva (transformation, wisdom, and liberation). Through the recitation of the Hanuman Chalisa, the devotee invites both energies into their life, enhancing their spiritual journey and protecting them from obstacles.

Esoteric Insight :

True spiritual growth happens when we integrate various divine forces within ourselves—courage from Hanuman and wisdom from Shiva—ultimately guiding us to divine fulfillment.

2. Shiva as the Source of All Auspiciousness

Lord Shiva is revered as the source of all good, auspicious, and spiritual energy in the universe. The verse implies that by reading the Hanuman Chalisa, the devotee becomes aligned with this powerful, auspicious energy, leading to an abundance of spiritual and material blessings.

Esoteric Insight :

Shiva's energy is transformative, purifying the devotee's heart and mind, enabling them to experience divine blessings in all areas of life.

Ramcharitmanas Connection

- Hanuman and Shiva's Connection :

In the Ramcharitmanas, Lord Hanuman is depicted as the greatest devotee of Lord Rama, and it is through his devotion that he receives immense spiritual power. His relationship with Lord Shiva is integral to his strength and wisdom, as both deities represent qualities that aid in spiritual transformation and growth.

- Shiva's Role in the Ramayana :

Though not directly involved in the Ramayana, Shiva's influence is acknowledged as being essential to the divine framework that governs the actions of other gods, including Hanuman.

Practical Application in Daily Life

1. Invoke Divine Blessings Through Recitation :

Make the recitation of the Hanuman Chalisa a regular practice. By doing so, you invite the divine presence of both Hanuman and Shiva into your life, helping to remove obstacles and guide you toward spiritual fulfillment.

2. Seek Spiritual Success :

True success is not just worldly achievement but spiritual growth. Align your actions with a higher purpose, and trust that the divine will guide you toward both material and spiritual fulfillment.

3. Embrace Transformation :

Like Lord Shiva, be open to transformation in your life. Let go of the past and embrace new beginnings with faith in the divine process of creation and destruction.

4. Cultivate Inner Strength and Wisdom :

Just as Hanuman exemplifies courage and strength, and Shiva embodies wisdom and transformation, work on developing both inner strength and wisdom. With these qualities, you can navigate the challenges of life with grace and purpose.

Conclusion

This Chaupai emphasizes the power of the Hanuman Chalisa to bring both material and spiritual success. By reciting this hymn with devotion, one is not only blessed by Lord Hanuman but also by Lord Shiva, the source of all auspiciousness. It highlights the spiritual connection between the two deities and their collective influence on the devotee's journey toward divine fulfillment and transformation.

Chaupai 40

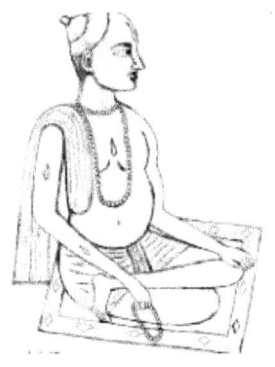

Tulsidas Sada Hari Chera,

Kijiye Nath Hriday Mam Dera.

तुलसीदास सदा हरि चेरा।

कीजै नाथ हृदय मम डेरा।।

Glossary of Key Awadhi Words

1. Tulsidas : Refers to Goswami Tulsidas, the great devotee and poet.

2. Sada : Always, forever, or constantly.

3. Hari : Lord, often referring to Lord Rama.

4. Chera : Servant or devotee; one who serves.

5. Kijiye : Make or do; here, it refers to asking or requesting.

6. Nath : Lord or Master, referring to Lord Rama.

7. Hriday : Heart.

8. Mam : My, referring to the speaker (Tulsidas) himself.

9. Dera : Dwelling, abode, or place of rest; in this context, it refers to seeking the Lord's presence in the heart.

Meaning of the Chaupai

"Tulsidas, always a servant of Lord Rama, asks that the Lord make His abode in his heart."

Hidden Spiritual Secrets

1. The Desire for Divine Presence

In this Chaupai, Tulsidas expresses his deep longing to have Lord Rama reside in his heart. He desires not just intellectual knowledge of the divine but the actual presence of the Lord within himself, symbolizing a deep and personal relationship with the divine.

Hidden Wisdom :

The heart, in spiritual terms, is often seen as the seat of devotion and the space where the divine can dwell. This verse reflects the profound desire for the Lord to occupy the core of one's being, making the heart His sacred abode.

Practical Insight :

To invite the divine into your life, cultivate a space of inner peace and devotion. Allow your heart to be a sanctuary for divine love, untainted by worldly distractions and desires.

2. Surrendering the Heart to the Divine

By requesting the Lord to make His abode in his heart, Tulsidas illustrates the concept of complete surrender. He seeks the presence of the divine not only in his mind but in the very essence of his being, showing that true devotion requires offering everything to the Lord.

Hidden Wisdom :

True devotion lies in offering your entire being—your thoughts, emotions, actions, and desires—to the divine. When the heart is surrendered, it becomes a pure vessel for divine grace.

Practical Insight :

In your daily life, practice surrender. Let go of the ego and personal attachments, allowing the divine to guide your thoughts and actions. Cultivate a heart filled with love, devotion, and humility.

3. Tulsidas's Role as the Eternal Servant

Tulsidas refers to himself as the "servant" or "Chera" of Lord Rama, a title he embraces with pride and humility. This reflects the highest form of devotion: to see oneself as the eternal servant of the divine, dedicated to serving the Lord without any expectation of reward.

Hidden Wisdom :

The role of a servant is not one of subjugation but of surrender and love. The servant's task is to serve with devotion and humility, recognizing the greatness of the master while remaining humble in their service.

Practical Insight :

Approach life with a servant's mindset. Serve others with humility, recognizing that each act of service is a way to serve the divine. Whether in work, family, or community, offer your actions as a form of worship.

Deeper Mystical Insights

1. The Heart as the Divine Temple

In many spiritual traditions, the heart is considered the temple of the divine. Tulsidas's plea to have Lord Rama dwell in his heart reflects the idea that the divine can be experienced when we purify and make space in our hearts for love and devotion.

Esoteric Insight :

When the heart is free from ego and worldly attachments, it becomes a place where the divine can reside. By focusing inward and purifying the heart, we can invite the presence of the divine into our lives.

2. Devotion as the Path to Divine Union

The verse illustrates that devotion is not just about external rituals but about creating an internal connection with the divine. Tulsidas's longing to have Rama reside within his heart is symbolic of the soul's yearning to unite with the divine.

Esoteric Insight :

True devotion leads to the union of the soul with the divine. It is a constant, loving connection, beyond rituals and external actions. This union brings inner peace and spiritual fulfillment.

Ramcharitmanas Connection

- Heart as the Seat of Devotion :

Throughout Ramcharitmanas, Tulsidas stresses that true devotion is not merely about external displays but about the internal, heartfelt connection with Lord Rama. This Chaupai reflects the central theme of his work: the importance of surrendering the heart and soul to the divine.

- Lord Rama's Abode in the Heart:

In the Ramcharitmanas, Lord Rama is often depicted as residing in the hearts of His devotees. By expressing the desire for Rama to reside in his own heart, Tulsidas aligns himself with this divine truth, offering himself as a humble servant in the service of the Lord.

Practical Application in Daily Life

1. Create Space for the Divine :

Make room for the divine in your heart by practicing love, kindness, and humility. Let go of negative emotions and attachments that prevent the Lord from dwelling in your heart.

2. Practice Surrender :

Surrender your ego, desires, and fears to the divine. Trust that by giving yourself fully to the divine will, you will experience peace and guidance in all aspects of life.

3. Live with Devotion :

Embody devotion in every action. Whether through prayer, service, or love, let each action be an offering to the divine. Recognize that the path of devotion leads to spiritual growth and fulfillment.

Conclusion

In this Chaupai, Tulsidas expresses his deep yearning for Lord Rama to reside in his heart. This verse is a reminder that true devotion is about inviting the divine into the core of our being, offering our entire selves in service to the Lord. Through humility, surrender, and unwavering devotion, we can cultivate a heart that is pure and open to divine grace.

Doha

Pavan Tanay Sankat Haran,

Mangal Murti Roop

Ram Lakhan Sita Sahit Hriday Basu Sur Bhoop.

पवन तनय संकट हरन,

मंगल मूर्ति रुप।

राम लखन सीता सहित,

हृदय बसहु सुर भूप।।

Glossary of Key Awadhi Words

1. Pavan Tanay : The son of the wind; referring to Hanuman, son of Vayu (Wind God).

2. Sankat Haran : Remover of troubles or difficulties.

3. Mangal Murti : Form of auspiciousness or good fortune.

4. Roop : Form or appearance.

5. Ram : Lord Rama, the seventh incarnation of Vishnu.

6. Lakhan : Lord Lakshman, brother of Lord Rama.

7. Sita : Goddess Sita, wife of Lord Rama.

8. Sahit : With, together.

9. Hriday : Heart.

10. Basu : Resides or dwells.

11. Sur Bhoop : King of the gods; referring to Lord Indra or the celestial rulers.

Meaning of the Chaupai

"O son of the wind, remover of troubles, you are the form of auspiciousness with the presence of Ram, Lakshman, and Sita together in your heart, and you dwell in the hearts of the divine kings."

Detailed Explanation of Key Phrases

1. Pavan Tanay Sankat Haran (Son of the Wind, Remover of Troubles)

- **Pavan Tanay :** Hanuman is known as the son of Vayu, the Wind God. Vayu represents speed, energy, and the life force. As the son of such a powerful deity, Hanuman inherits extraordinary strength, agility, and divine energy.

- **Sankat Haran :** This phrase means that Hanuman is the remover of obstacles and troubles. He alleviates suffering and dispels difficulties from the lives of those who call upon him with faith. His divine power is activated through devotion and service to Lord Rama, enabling him to conquer challenges that seem insurmountable.

Hidden Wisdom:

This line highlights Hanuman's power to clear obstacles, both physical and mental. His divine heritage allows him to be an eternal source of support for devotees, helping them overcome their struggles.

Practical Insight :

Whenever you face challenges, call upon the strength and grace of Hanuman. Devote yourself to positive action and trust in his ability to help you navigate through hardships, as his power transcends all difficulties.

2. Mangal Murti Roop (Form of Auspiciousness and Good Fortune)

- **Mangal Murti :** Hanuman is described here as the "Mangal Murti," which means he is the embodiment of good fortune and auspiciousness. Everything about him—his form, actions, and presence—is considered auspicious and brings positive energy into the lives of his devotees.

- **Roop :** The word "Roop" refers to Hanuman's divine form. His appearance is not just physical but carries a spiritual significance—radiating purity, strength, and divine grace. His form is considered to be a source of blessings and protection.

Hidden Wisdom :

Hanuman, as the "Mangal Murti," represents the power of auspiciousness. The divine energy he embodies can transform adverse situations into positive ones when approached with true devotion. His very presence in the lives of devotees is a symbol of blessings and divine favor.

Practical Insight :

Seek to embody Hanuman's qualities of strength, humility, and devotion in your life. By doing so, you can attract good fortune and ensure that your actions and decisions align with the divine will. Stay grounded in purpose, and invoke auspiciousness through prayer and positive deeds.

3. Ram Lakhan Sita Sahit Hriday Basu Sur Bhoop (With Ram, Lakshman, and Sita in His Heart, He Dwells in the Hearts of the Divine Kings)

- Ram, Lakshman, and Sita Sahit : Hanuman is not just a servant of Lord Rama, but he holds the divine trio—Rama, Lakshman, and Sita—within his heart. This signifies that Hanuman's heart is filled with divine love, as he is dedicated to the service of Rama, the embodiment of righteousness; Lakshman, the loyal brother; and Sita, the symbol of purity and devotion.

- **Hriday Basu :** His heart, therefore, is the dwelling place of these divine qualities. In this phrase, "Basu" means to reside or dwell, indicating that Hanuman holds these virtues within him at all times.

- **Sur Bhoop :** The "Sur Bhoop" refers to the divine kings, like Lord Indra, who are the rulers of the heavens. Hanuman's divine presence in their hearts symbolizes that he is revered by the celestial beings. His unwavering devotion to Lord Rama has earned him a place of honor not only on Earth but also in the divine realms.

Hidden Wisdom :

Hanuman's heart is not just the dwelling place of Lord Rama but also a beacon of divine qualities such as strength, purity, and devotion. This suggests that when you fill your heart with these virtues, you too can attract the blessings of the gods and live a life aligned with divine purpose.

Practical Insight :

Work to cultivate a heart filled with love, devotion, and righteousness. Just as Hanuman's heart is a temple for the divine, your heart can become a source of divine connection and strength. Seek alignment with higher virtues, and you will naturally earn divine blessings and guidance.

Deeper Mystical Insights

1. Hanuman as the Divine Protector

Hanuman's dual role as both a remover of obstacles (Sankat Haran) and an embodiment of auspiciousness

(Mangal Murti) underscores his role as the divine protector. Through his grace, obstacles are removed, and divine blessings are bestowed, creating a balanced and protected life for his devotees.

2. Heart as the Temple of Divine Presence

The fact that Hanuman holds the divine trio—Rama, Lakshman, and Sita—in his heart teaches us that the heart, when pure and devoted, becomes the seat of divine power. Through devotion, one can invite the divine into their inner being and, by extension, their life.

3. The Celestial Blessing

The fact that Hanuman is revered by the gods and resides in their hearts highlights the deep spiritual connection he shares with the divine realms. It suggests that by living with devotion and purity, a devotee can earn favor not only from earthly figures but from the entire cosmic order.

Ramcharitmanas Connection

- The Divine Form of Hanuman :

Hanuman's description as the "Mangal Murti" aligns with his portrayal in Ramcharitmanas as the ideal devotee, pure and selfless. Tulsidas repeatedly emphasizes that Hanuman's greatness lies in his heart, filled with devotion to Lord Rama. This verse reinforces that Hanuman's purity and service make him a beacon of divine grace and auspiciousness.

- Hanuman's Role as the Bridge Between Mortal and Divine :

Hanuman's relationship with Rama, Lakshman, and Sita is central to his role as the bridge between the mortal and divine realms. This verse exemplifies how Hanuman embodies the virtues of these divine figures, offering an example for all devotees to emulate.

Practical Application in Daily Life

1. Fill Your Heart with Virtues :

Like Hanuman, strive to fill your heart with devotion, purity, and strength. Let these virtues guide your actions, and they will bring divine blessings into your life.

2. Seek Divine Blessings Through Service :

Hanuman's devotion to Rama teaches us that service to the divine and others brings auspiciousness into our lives. Act with selflessness and devotion, and divine blessings will follow.

3. Align Your Actions with Divine Will :

As Hanuman resides in the hearts of the gods, aim to align your actions with divine will. When your actions reflect the higher virtues of love, strength, and purity, you too can earn divine favor.

Conclusion

This Doha emphasizes Hanuman's divine nature and his unwavering devotion to Lord Rama. It teaches us that when we fill our hearts with purity, devotion, and divine virtues, we become aligned with the divine will and open ourselves to blessings and protection from both earthly and celestial realms.

www.ingramcontent.com/pod-product-compliance
Lightning Source LLC
LaVergne TN
LVHW061609070526
838199LV00078B/7221